How Black Were Our Valleys

A BBTS Publication
Deri, Bargoed.
BBTS (BaarBaaraTheSheep Publishers Est. 2012)

© Butts-Thompson and Price 2013/1014
First Published February 2014

ISBN-13: 978-1495399497

ISBN-10: 1495399494

CreateSpace: ISBN registered with BooksInPrint.com®

Cover Design: © Butts-Thompson and Price
Typeset: Georgia and Arial

How Black Were Our Valleys

A 30 Year Commemoration of the 1984/85 Miners' Strike.

By

Deborah Price and Natalie Butts – Thompson

Contents

Introduction - Background

Dedication

Acknowledgments

Foreword

Introduction

How Black Were

Our Valleys

The inspiration for the book came after hearing a speech given by Ron Stoate at The Newbridge Hotel on 17th April 2013.

It was a Miners Beneficiary on the day of Thatcher's funeral. Ron's talk was emotive, shocking and informative it brought tears to many eyes. Afterwards we approached him and asked if any of his stories had been recorded. Ron told us that he had been approached many times over the years, with a view to producing a book, but nothing had ever come of it. Realising the 30th anniversary of the strike was next year, we took this opportunity to arrange a meeting with Ron and thus began our rewarding project.

Natalie Butts-Thompson

I decided to co-write this book in memory of the 1984 strike, because I believe there is not enough personal history recorded about the event. The strike was an important part of Welsh History. When Margaret Thatcher passed away, children, including my own, were asking; 'Who is Margaret Thatcher?' They have no knowledge of the hardship and poverty that was handed to the mining communities by Thatcher in 1984 even though there is a high probability that most of the children's grandfathers or great grandfathers were involved in the strike.

The interview process: collecting, editing and publishing of the book has taken me on my own personal journey down memory lane, I originate from a mining family and although only nine at the time, I have many memories of the strike. I have shed tears and gasped in horror at some of the stories we have heard along the way.

Deborah Price

As part of our second year History Degree at the University of South Wales, we were required to undertake some kind of work placement using skills necessary for an historian. Natalie's family has a history of mining and with the 30th anniversary of the 1984/85 strike looming and our interest in Welsh local history, we decided to undertake this collection of memories and events that we feel deserve to be heard. The 1984/85 strike was one of the longest and hardest in history and should be remembered and recognized as such for future generations.

Background Information

Trade Union membership was at its highest in the late 1970's
The importance of the NUM related to its power.

After the mine closures of the 1960s the trade union had been largely ignored as a source of influence within British politics. However this was all changed by OPEC. In 1972, under a Tory Government, the coal miners launched a national strike over wages that had a significant effect upon electricity supplies. The strike was eventually settled after a National inquiry that decided firmly in favour of the trade union's demand.

A further Strike followed in 1974 during which the Prime Minister Edward Heath determined to settle, 'who runs the country' called a general election, which he lost. Under the new Labour Government the NUM was ascendant and with it a new form of class politics was emerging, with new and unusual organised forms of solidarity action. (Beynon, Engaging Labour. p.12)

In 1983 the coal miners elected a new President. Arthur Scargill was President of the Yorkshire Area of the NUM. Before joining the Labour Party, Scargill had been a young communist and had been active in the strikes of 1972 and 1974. He, along with many other young miners had attended courses at Leeds University and had been influenced by the teaching and writings of Vic Allen.

In debates in the early eighties with Ken Coates and others Scargill had made clear his disagreements with the Institute of Workers' Control. In his view alternative planning only succeeded in drawing the trade union into the employers' realm. The way forward, in his view, was to challenge the employer and the state with trade union power. He had evidence to support this.

In 1981, when factories were being closed all over the old industrial districts, the National Coal Board announced its intention to close coal mines. This provoked immediate strike action in South Wales, followed sporadically across the other coal fields. In the face of this reaction the closures were withdrawn.

Three years later, however it was a different story, with a more confident Thatcher government (after victory in the South Atlantic and in the general election) and a well prepared state. The NUM supported a dispute over mine closures that rolled through each of its Areas. Federal in structure, the national union's executive supported the developing strike and resisted calls for a national ballot (see: Beynon, 1985).

The issues here were complex, undoubtedly the decision became a source of argument and criticism of the union. The strike lasted a year and ended with the NUM recommending a return to work 'without an agreement' in March 1985. Before the strike erupted the NUM had learned many lessons from the closure of the manufacturing plants.

The miners' union employed research and education officers who linked with groups in the universities to produce documents for a *Campaign for Coal.* The logic of the Campaign centred on the need to build a broad based coalition of support for the coalminers in their defence of jobs. It produced a series of discussion papers held together in large maroon envelope folders.

In this way, details of employment multipliers and the impact of closures on local communities were brought together with papers dealing with energy policy and the threats posed by nuclear reactors. They formed the basis for discussions around endless evening meetings across the coalfields of the UK and were helpful in producing extremely well informed cadres of local activists capable of arguing and debating the case for keeping coal mines open. They also extended the campaign beyond the coalfields and the strike itself produced a multiplicity of 'twinning' arrangements between the mining towns and villages and other local groups and communities – sociology departments figured centrally in this. Ultimately the strike was sustained through coordinated community activity and women were centrally involved and critical to this.(Ibid. pp.16/17)

A word from Dr. Conchar – Conker Books online;

"My funniest memory of the strike was dancing the Conga around Sheffield City Hall on a Saturday night, after a Women Against Pit Closures conference – Arthur Scargill led the dance, I was near the back and there were several hundred miners' wives in between us."

Our good friend Alan Conchar unfortunately passed away on the 12th November 2013. Alan came to Cardiff to attend University over twenty years ago and stayed. He visited his family regularly who still live in Dumfries and Galloway, he had very strong political views and took part in many rallies and demonstrations over the years. He was a staunch supporter of the miners' strike and was looking forward to the publication of this book.

R I P. Alan, we miss you.

Dedication

We would like to dedicate this book to all of the strong minded ladies in the valleys who stood tall against Thatcher and never gave up, including Natalie's very own Iron Ladies, her mother and late grandmother Sylvia Butts. Sylvia was a strong hard working lady who worked around the clock arranging food parcels, trips for the kids and toys at Christmas, she also found the time to join the men on the picket line.

We would also like to dedicate it to the miners, strong hard working men, who stood united and fought so hard to secure jobs for future generations. You are the true heroes and may the memory of the strike of 1984/85 live on.

Let us not forget to give thanks for the generosity of those that supported the miners and their families throughout those dark times. Aid was received from many quarters, not just from this country; it came from abroad, a variety of different industries, a very diverse set of groups and numerous individuals. The strike would not have endured without their help.

Acknowledgements

We would like to thank everybody who contributed to the success of this publication, everyone gave their time, effort and encouragement freely and enthusiastically to enable us to complete the book in the short time that we had available. Huge thanks to all our contributors, especially Ron Stoate whose inspirational speech was the gateway to the book.

Also to Ian Jenkins (Deborah's partner) for his knowledge of Welsh History, driving us to places we may never have found on our own and for numerous cups of tea whilst being ignored all day long. To Colin Thomas for his research and internet links and recommending names for interviews.

To Reg Malpass, Gayle O'Dare, Cynon Valley remembered, Carol White and Ceri Thompson, National Museum Wales-Big Pit for photographic use. To The Socialist Party of Great Britain who let us use some of their pamphlet text. To Dr. Alex Clayton, head of film at Bristol University for the use of "All Out." To Professor Huw Beynon, author of "Digging Deeper" for allowing use of the information in his book and paper.

To Mrs. Fay Swain from Deri for the loan of Penallta. To Dr. Lynda Evans, for agreeing to provide our foreword and Dr. Jonathon Durrant, for agreeing to our project in the first place, both work for The University of South Wales. To Michael O'Brien, author of; 'Prisons Exposed' and 'The Death of Justice' for recommending us to his publisher.

Foreword

I am privileged to have been asked by Debbie Price and Natalie Butts-Thompson to write the foreword for their book "How Black Were Our Valleys". I first met Debbie two years ago during our campaign to oppose the development of a massive incinerator in our locality and was impressed with her determination and commitment to champion the cause for the local community. Since then Debbie has continued to contribute to ensuring the voice of local people is heard through her poetry and writing.

Natalie herself experienced the 1984/85 strike as a child, both her father and grandfather were miners and her mother and grandmother helped to set up The Penrhiwceiber Womens' Support Group.

As a miner's daughter born and bred in a mining village, I am acutely aware of the legacy coal mining has left within the now redundant coalfields in Britain. However, the coal fields of South Wales now lie silent and the landscape is once again becoming green across some areas of the Valleys. Many people have paid a high price for the mining of coal and we have much to thank them for. Some of their stories are told within this book. I am immensely proud of the heritage we have within the South Wales Valleys and we must never forget how coalmining put South Wales at the forefront of industry.

I commend Debbie and Natalie's book to you. You will find it interesting, upsetting, funny and nostalgic.

Dr Linda Evans MBA;Dip HRM;BEd

Ron Stoate

Photo: Socialist Party.org taken at The Newbridge Hotel, 17th April 2013

Ron was elected Chairman of the N.U.M. in South Wales in 1991, previously holding the position of Lodge Secretary at Penallta which closed its doors in November 1991. Ron had worked there for 11 years and previously at Brittania for 14 years. It was his speech that inspired the idea of this commemorative book. Ron now works as official caretaker at the Num in Pontypridd.

Ron's speech at The Newbridge Hotel on the 17th April 2013, was just one of many, he has given over the years.

Before the official strike was called meetings were tense. I knew a strike was coming. The experiences of the 1972/74 strikes were still fresh in my memory, back then I hadn't had any experience of strike action and I remember how hard it had been just to keep the house warm. I really hadn't known what to do and didn't want to go through it all again. Those strikes had lasted 6 weeks and 3 months, nobody had any idea of the new challenges that lay ahead.

What I had learned from 1972/74 was that if you needed to heat the house you did it by any means possible. This time around I would go and chop a tree down if necessary, as well as going picking coal.

I had a wife and two small children to look after. Some boys from Caerphilly told me about 'The Nantgarw cutting,' it was full of waste coke. My brother borrowed a neighbour's estate car and he'd go and fill it. He'd have to come back up the A470 as the car wouldn't get up the hill it was so packed. Only two people could go, so that there was more room for the coke, we shared it with everyone back home.

I went with him once and it was so cold I couldn't feel my hands or lift anything after a while. My brother used to lift the big bags into the car for me. When we got home we'd give everyone a bag each. In those days we needed the coal to get hot water.

(Coal central heating was provided by the NCB and would be paid for by a 4% levy from wages.) Some individual mines were allowed to keep producing coal for schools, hospitals and for the old people.

Picketing

We were lucky enough to have the use of Ystrad Stute for the Penallta pits office; this gave us the use of phones and a place to employ proper managerial skills in order to send the boys picketing. Shamrock buses were hiring vehicles to the N.U.M. to take pickets to various collieries, at the time I recall the owner claiming that his phone was being tapped. Nobody believed it, we thought it was paranoia, but of course, back then we didn't realise just how important the knowledge of our whereabouts was.

3

At Rose Heyworth Colliery in Abertillery, all the traffic was held up by strikers. Looking behind us we heard the police asking everyone to clear the road, I shouted; "Don't listen to them; we're here to block the road, that's why we're here!" The police responded by linking arms in an 'arrow head' shape, they then stamped through us with little steps.

Photograph of Rose Heyworth Colliery courtesy of People's Collection Wales

I got picked up by the police that day just because I'd opened my mouth. The two policemen who picked me up, dropped me, then one of them tried to knee me, he partly missed but I was so angry I did it back to him. Another policeman came and took a photograph, but I made a face so that I couldn't get recognised. I was then thrown into the van head first.

That day, me and my brother got locked up, we weren't let out until the next day. When we went to court, the magistrate was sympathetic; the police had apparently lied about what I had supposedly said. The magistrate, who was an old lady fined me £100 and said "Mr. Stoate, I hope it will be all over for you soon."

Up in North Wales, Bersham Colliery came out on strike, but they wouldn't picket Point of Ayr as it was still working. We in South Wales had to organise picketing from down here. There was a bus rota of thirteen men at a time; it was too far away to go every day, so we stayed for a week. I believe two of the men actually remained there.

People would put you up in their houses for a week in North Wales and usually about two or three days at a time in the Midlands. Surprisingly many of these people had no association with the pits, but they were still generous enough to help us. People all over were supporting us, by giving us places to stay, sometimes you wouldn't even meet the people, you were just given the keys and told to make yourself at home.

One bloke in North Wales said "Don't worry about the dog, the doors open, go in and help yourselves," then he just drove off. There were five of us, we couldn't get over how trustworthy he was. The previous night we had stayed on the floor of the community centre and we were gagging for a cup of tea, but we felt embarrassed going through his cupboards, we did in the end though. Another time he came home and we were all sat round eating bread and cheese (each man picketing was allocated a subsidy of £7 outside your area, or £5 inside your area) so we had a little money for food, the guy said "Don't bother with that," he opened a chest freezer which was full to the brim with meat, he kept his own pigs.

When the annual demonstration through Tolpuddle to celebrate 'The Tolpuddle Martyrs' was arranged, we got together a bus load of fifty, going on the Saturday, ready for the Sunday. When we got there we were taken to the labour club, where people were bidding on you to take you home with them. Myself and a mate were taken to this blokes house, which was the scruffiest house I had ever seen.

There was a lean-to at the back of the house, falling to bits. Everything was painted bright red; in the room was a church pew and a camp bed for me to sleep on, while Kevin slept in their little girl's room. They didn't have much, but what little they had they shared with us. The room was full of books and magazines, turned out both people were really educated, whilst she was still at university, he had written a book about numbers, each number representing something, up to splitting the atom.

Closer to home; at Penallta pit there was a mass picket on the gate; I was vice lodge at the time. Two policemen drove through the picket line with a miner smuggled in the back of their car (we found out later he was from Nelson.) Fuming, I went to see the manager to tell him to get the police off the premises. I was told "Don't turn the pit into a battleground," as far as I was concerned they had already done that by involving the police. I was so angry I picked up a chair and threw it, there was a bit of a rumpus outside the lamp room, but I hurt myself more than anything.

Pickets at Penallta, photograph courtesy of The National Museum of Wales, Big Pit, Blaenavon.

The media became involved and would report that; 'we've got the men back!' when in actual fact there were only one or two men in attendance. This propaganda needed to be nipped in the bud. There were photo's of loaded coal on the weighbridge at Ystrad Mynach with one of the men that went back, but mostly they were just in a room reading, so that it could be reported they were present.

One day I was arrested outside Llanwern, lucky for me there was an amateur photographer present, who was a miner from the coke-works. He had been taking photos that the press wouldn't take. This time he'd taken a photograph of thousands of police helmets on the grass, which had been removed in preparation for a confrontation. He came to court with me over that one. Over a twelve month I was arrested four times in total, eventually I was put on a curfew so that I couldn't go picketing.

Part of my bail conditions and many others in the same situation was that you could only picket in your own place of work. Myself and two of my brothers had to go to the station and report twice a day, in effect preventing us from going anywhere else.

My experience was that the police used their authority to bully the pickets, but only when there were more police than pickets. Mostly they would engage in general chit-chat and be friendly towards us.

Orgreave was the worst experience, we had to be taken there, or we would never have found the place. The coke works were down in a dip, and we could not believe how many police were present, their intention was to make the miner's look bad. There were twelve or thirteen Welshmen, Billy Greenaway, from Cefn Forest, who worked for the transport side, ended up with a broken collarbone after being smacked with a truncheon.

There were middle aged guys who could not seem to get away from the fighting. Some of us got locked up in Strangeways prison but fortunately the staff there were very supportive. All the charges were settled out of court, even though they were serious rioting charges. There were police from all areas coming into court, but, their statements were contradictory, as they hadn't had the chance to collude. Their aim had been to make an example of some of the pickets.

Apart from one comment from my father-in-law six about six months into the strike, when he told me; "Don't you think you should leave it there now?" I had no grief off any other family members, my mother, my wife and her relatives were all very supportive. No thought of going back ever entered my mind, never would I cross a picket line. Striking became a way of life. It was hard though, getting up at 3 or 4am in one of the hardest winters I had experienced. We were picketing outside, with a sleeve for a bobble hat to try and keep warm. It was just like getting up and going to work, there was always a feeling that you were needed in a certain place, at a certain time and that was that.

Support

The support that we received from all over the country and from abroad, undoubtedly kept us going as long as we did. Ystrad Stute was used as a distribution point for food that had been collected locally and donated.

I remember around Christmas time, the unions had bought a load of old scrawny chickens; there wasn't a lot on them to go round.

Fortunately for us, aid came from Belgium and France in the form of more than twenty, quickly defrosting turkeys. They needed to be distributed straight quickly and deciding who were the most worthy recipients was a hard choice. One guy, Dai, I think his name was, was really offended when offered one, he was single and told us to give it to a family, even though he had nothing.

The food delivery boys told me about the time when some people from Austria and France visited. They were interested in seeing the distribution and collection processes for themselves. How the food was divided equally and fairly amongst the community. They were given token gifts of miner's badges and other memorabilia to take home with them. At the airport, on their return home, they were searched and questioned. They were given the third degree to try and frighten them off I guess and probably to stop them coming back. Also, sadly, all their gifts were taken from them.

The summer of 1984, brought some relief to the lucky families who were offered a holiday by the Irish equivalent of; The Transport and General Workers' Union. I was on bail at the time so I was there with my wife. They arranged a trip for fifty kids and twelve adults; we were split into two groups, Dublin and Monahan. It was at the time that America wanted to come into Northern Ireland, so we had to fly to Southern Ireland and cross the border in.

In Dublin the group was taken to The Phoenix Park Zoo, when workers in the zoo found out who they were, they did a collection for them. When we arrived in Monahan the community centre was open and food and drink was laid out for everyone. Every single day they took the kids out on excursions, canoeing and outward-bounding, it was brilliant.

When we returned home I wrote a thank you letter, I still

remember the address today, '11 Coolock Street, Coolock.' I received a card in return with a donkey on the cover, standing outside a pub. Inside was a tenner, the message read: "Don't be like the donkey, go inside."

Returning to Work

At the end of the strike a group of men came down from Kent, there had been twenty men sacked in Snowdon, apparently they had spread the word that the pit was flooding. This was nonsense; they got sacked because they had gone down illegally to check if the pit was alright. The area director was refusing to reinstate anyone who was sacked during the strike. The Kent boys came down to picket with us, the stance was to fight for the sacked miners once we were back in work.

By now the men were resigned to going back to work, the unions had agreed, the unions didn't want to agree to this new picket, so they agreed not to. Penallta went back to work as a whole body of workers, but we went back one day late, because the Kent boys had picketed with us on the official return day and were staying at my house, so I felt I had duty to

14

look after them. They actually ended up staying another night after I returned because they had a march in London the next day. Disappointingly, just one official came out clapping the day we marched back into work, the rest were pretty sheepish.

After twelve months it was really hard to get back into work, I was asked to carry a bucket in only to find that the coal face had dropped. This was a huge health and safety issue and needed to be rectified before we could start work again.

There were many questions I wanted to ask the chairman of the coal board, Robert Aslam, such as 'What was going to happen now?' but he refused to meet me in the lamp room, as did other officials and N.A.C.O.D.S. I had only wanted to ask about the future of the pit, but properly, across the table, they all refused. There was no reason why we shouldn't have been producing coal well into the next century. But by now I was resigned to the fact that the pits would go, I just didn't expect 'The Domino effect.' After the strike, the N.U.M. were presented with a plaque and the key to Cardiff City, because we had been refused permission to march there during the strike by the 'Tory government.

On the day Penallta closed in November 1991, we presented miners' lamps to Michael Foot, Paul Murphy and Kim Howells, even though the latter had slagged us off on the radio during an interview with Patrick Sissens. Then we all marched out together, Ron Davies was there and he was fully aware of what we were going to do. When Tower colliery was threatened after Penallta I went to support them, Ron Davies was there too and he didn't even bother to speak to me.

We would still have gone on strike even if we had known the pits would close eventually. When the pits were around it was like a natural progression, everybody went to work there, there was work guaranteed for everyone. The conversation and the social life in our communities revolved around the mines.

Even though the work was hard and often dangerous, everyone had a sense of pride. Things were structured; there were jobs for everyone, not just on the coal face. There were apprenticeships and occasionally the opportunity for early retirement. All that is gone now, there are no jobs. At the age of forty two trying to gain employment was hard, I was treated with contempt, just for having to sign on the dole temporarily.

I had to experience fifteen years of doing different jobs and I am

a bitter man, even today.

Penallta, the last deep mine of the Rhymney Valley, just prior to closure

1991, it was an open day for the miners' families who were allowed to visit

pit-bottom, No.1 shaft. Photograph courtesy of Reg Malpass 'the reggy –

flickr' who worked at Penallta as a trainee mine surveyor in 1954.

David Griffiths

David worked as a miner and as part of the mines rescue team in Taff Merthyr Colliery which was sunk in 1924, it finally closed its doors on 30th October 1992. David was forced to retire, not through choice, but from an horrific accident underground in which he saved the life of a young lad and took the brunt of a collapse leaving himself severely injured.

David unfolded his story to us as if it only happened yesterday, his memory is crisp and his emotions are still raw.

Strike Action

Myself and my workmates were called into a meeting at Taff Lodge on a Sunday, it was March 1984, the agenda was 'Strike.' My butty, one of the contractors, put up his hand during the meeting and asked the question; "Why should we have to go on strike?" he kept on even though people were speaking over him, the union didn't want to listen.

Although we were given a vote and three quarters of us voted not to strike, it seemed inevitable that a strike was on the cards. Even though we had voted to go into work the next day, if our pit was picketed there would not be many that would cross the picket line. Lo and behold when we turned up for work the next day, miner's from Penrhiwceiber Colliery were there on the picket line.

I would never cross a picket line, as far as I'm concerned we all looked out for each other underground and we must all stand united over-ground. The strike had started, unfortunately not one single miner who stood outside their colliery's that day could imagine the devastating hardship and poverty that they would endure during this lengthy strike. Most thought it would be a couple of weeks, but Mrs.Thatcher would not give in.

As days moved into weeks the picketing escalated, 'The Flying Pickets' as we were now called, moved from town to town bringing the mines to a halt.

When picketing over on Fochriw mountain at the small Taylor

Woodrow mine, there were only three of us, it was freezing cold, but we did have a little caravan to make tea in.

I was asked to stay the night, but the only place to sleep was an old barn with a trough in it, I bagged the trough, (laughing) at least it was off the floor.

Another time I remember going down to Port Talbot steelworks, what a day that was. We couldn't go the normal route as police were barricading, so we had to go over the mountain. Our clapped out mini-bus weren't the best, it broke down half way there and we had to push it for about twenty minutes. We got stopped by the police; we then tried to convince them that we were going fishing. There wasn't a fishing rod in sight and a bus crammed with miners, we were not believed.

We were met at the steelworks by a massive crowd of miners and of course the Thames Valley Police who were all around six foot six in height. Needless to say, scuffles broke out between the police and the Miners. Every time lorries came out I witnessed miners linking arms and running as a tribe, knocking over every policeman in their way.

The police would respond by hitting the miners with their wooden truncheons, grabbing them and throwing them in the back of the wagons, where they would have a beating, when they were seen the miners would shake the wagon to try and get them out. We miners gave as good as we got mind, as far as we were concerned we were there to do a job and win our fight then get back to work as soon as possible.

The police were enjoying it, they were getting paid double time for their favours to Maggie and they let the miners know this by pinning twenty pound notes to their vans. That was very frustrating for us Miners who didn't have two pennies to rub together. They were petty as well; I witnessed a man getting arrested for merely cleaning his fingernails with a lollipop stick, the police claiming that it could have been used for an offensive weapon. Another man got arrested just because of his name, Tracy Pickett, the policeman said "And I'm Errol Flynn," later they confirmed that it was his real name.

I got into a few scrapes myself mind, my first arrest was at the steelworks, a copper was grabbing me to put me in the van and the other miners were pulling me the other way, before I knew it I was wrestling three policemen. I got locked in the cells overnight and also had a ticking off from my big brother, I believe his words were "you're a handy bugger, all I could see on the T.V. was you fighting three coppers," as my wrestling match had made the six o'clock news. After reading me the riot act he offered me a job on a house he'd just bought. Me and my Dad did help him out but we wouldn't take any money, just a couple of beers.

As the weeks turned into months, frustration grew on the picket lines. More and more police were drafted in and even though the government strongly denied it, many miners believe the army were also on the picket lines. I saw it with my own eyes, a miner on a picket line with me spotted his own son, who was supposedly in the army fighting for his country, but was instead on the picket lines fighting against the miners, he was horrified. Many miners families were torn apart by these actions, this man would never speak to his son again. In the Valleys we were pretty tight; however, some scabs did cross the picket line.

These scabs were outcasted by their communities, even today they are still scabs and they will always be scabs.

Surviving the Strike

David and Christine's expressions tell this part of their story, there is a great sadness in both their faces and you can tell that the experience took its toll on both of them.

We just survived, Christine had a small job in the butchers and she would share her wage with my family and hers. We would collect a parcel from the Ceiber Hall on a Thursday and I would go over to the Cwm Cynon with my nylon sacks and a shopping trolley pinched from Tesco's to collect coal for me and my mother.

The winter was horrendous that year; however spirits were high over the tip. We were not safe from the police either, we would hear them coming. Then you could see the men popping their heads out of their holes like meer-cats and running over the bridge with whatever coal they had managed to scavenge.

We even went pinching in the phurnacite, we had to avoid the police on the gates mind, I remember there was one scab working there at the time. It was pretty awful, didn't know where I was going, and kept on falling down holes all the time. I worked very hard that day for half a bag of coal. The police used to say "Carry on boys; we're all on double time."

My mother enjoyed the challenges of collecting food for everyone, she used to like going around meeting people. The women used to go around the shops and collect donations and they would have a big barbeque at the Cwm. They would put on a fun day for the whole community. There would be a jazz band playing and there was always plenty of food for everyone.

Coming up to Christmas, I decided, 'Shit or bust' I had to go and see the bank manager. I had no money and was already slightly overdrawn. I gave him a sob story, including the fact that my mother wasn't well, to my surprise he said as I was a loyal customer he'd wipe out the overdraft and lend me five hundred pounds. I though it was wonderful, I gave my Mum three hundred pounds.

Going back to Work

It came to a point when we knew the fight was over; there was no way Thatcher was going to back down. Thatcher didn't want to happen to her what had happened in 1974 under the Heath government, there would be no power cuts this time around. Thatcher had anticipated Scargill's moves and had been stockpiling coal for a long time. She called the miners 'The Enemy Within.'

' In the Falklands we had to fight the enemy without. Here the enemy is within...'

Margaret Thatcher, 19 July 1984

This snapshot was taken from the lost video "All Out",

I marched back to work that day with a heavy heart, I felt like a year had been wasted for nothing. The Miner's were badly in debt, the ones who lived in pit houses owed a years rent, plus all their other bills. I knew the pits would not be around for much longer. Money had been withheld by the benefit system and National Insurance hadn't been paid, so if they had a bump they wouldn't be covered. It was £1.50 per week to cover and being in the rescue team I needed to be covered. There was a lot of bad feeling between the officials and the men.

The Aftermath

I think mine closures affected other employers in the area; local industries and shops needed the business off the Miner's to succeed. Community spirit disappeared, except amongst the older generation. There are drink and drug problems. If the mines were around now I think the Valleys would be different, without a doubt. There would be jobs for the kids and there would not be so many boarded up houses in our area.

Given half a chance I would go back down the pit

tomorrow. Although it was a bad year for all the Miner's, not just in the South Wales Valley's, it was also a good year, in that you can look back and remember, not just with sorrow, but with pride, the whole of the Valley's uniting together. Community spirit and morale was excellent. The women were the back-bone of the men, collecting the parcels, issuing food and even picketing. The men could not have survived the year without their women.

Food parcels packed and ready to be given out to the mining community in Penrhiwceiber. Photograph courtesy of Gayle O'Dare: Cynon Valley Remembered.

David Davies (aka Ropey)

Dai whilst speaking at Aberdare during the strike.

Dai lives in Penrhiwceiber with his wife Linda and is still running the Penrhiwceiber Institute today. During the strike a group of students from Bristol University, made a video called "All Out" recording the Penrhiwceiber women's group. David had a copy of this video which we had been unsuccessful in locating until we mentioned it the day we interviewed him. We contacted Bristol University who have now added it to their archives after we converted it to DVD format. We have been given permission to use the video, who's transcript is contained later in the book, for a 30th anniversary commemorative afternoon at Big Pit in 2014.

In March 1984 the decision to strike was being debated, there was a list of twenty six pits destined for closure, we were unsure about Nantgarw as it was a cosmopolitan pit, but on Monday 6th March Nantgarw came out with us. We knew there was going to be a battle, Nottingham weren't keen to come out, maybe if more of them had it would have made a difference. In Penrhiwceiber our union committee was 24 strong, this included one delegate from every part of the pit. This was our 'Collective' against the N.C.B.

Thatcher definitely had it in for the miners, Scargill was the only one with the guts to come out against her. After the 1972 and 1974 strikes, we had invited Scargill down to the Cynon and Rhondda Valleys and had good relationships with him. The Tories didn't like the Trade Unions and even though there were many ex-servicemen working in the pits, 75%, in 1959, when I started work on the coalface, she still inferred that they were 'The Enemy Within.' Thatcher's saying "I'll never go through the side door," backfired on her after a speech in Swansea Pavilion, she had no choice but to leave through the back door.

The reality of Picketing

We were all over the place picketing, so I was away from home a lot and I had a wife and four children to support. One of my boys was working as a miner so he was on strike with me too. We went up to Point of Ayr for weeks at a time trying to convert the lads who were still working. There were police in plain clothes egging on the miners to have a confrontation with police who were in uniform. Travelling up to North Wales we used to have a laugh though, we'd keep spirits up by shouting things like "Mint sauce yer bastards," at the sheep, I think we all would have liked a lamb chop for dinner back then.

Pickets in Cilfynydd and Pontypridd were getting picked on by the police for niggly things and were continuously being asked to produce their driving licences for no reason. The police went out of their way to shut down villages, stopping traffic to pits and other places of work also. Outside the lodge gates there was a box, Harry Baker had a snake and he used to rise it up in relation to those going past the picket line.

A bus load of us went up to Orgreave, we stayed on the floor in the miners club. The media propaganda showed the miners rushing at the police, when in reality the reverse was true. The police had dogs on extending leads; many lads got nasty bites on their legs. The media mostly portrayed the miners as thugs.

In Aug/Sept of 1984 we were told that the lights were going to go out, but it was untrue. Thatcher and her Tory government had made sure that a repeat of 72'74 would not happen by stockpiling coal and oil a long time before the strike had even started. Kim Howells said "You should consider going back to work," his actions led to commandeering the cranes down in Swansea. He was only appointed as a research officer, he shouldn't have spoken. He sent us to picket a power station that had been closed for ten years, what sort of research was that?

Support

My daughter got married during the strike, everybody rallied around to get food for a party in the house. It was great success. The younger people who were trying to buy their houses had it the hardest, trying to keep up payments on their mortgages was a struggle. Social security benefits were a daunting task for many, but there was one social security officer who helped out by showing people how to fill out the forms the right way to make a successful claim.

We had tremendous support from The Bristol West, Labour Party, which was an affluent area. Every Sunday a car would turn up at the lodge full of food and supplies from Bristol. Our Lodge office was right outside the pit gates, so we had control; it was unusual in its location and the fact that we owned it.

There was also a Penrhiwceiber Women's support group started by the late Barbara Curtis. This group took a lot of the worry away from the men as they were in charge of providing food. The Penrhiwceiber banner's motto was "Knowledge is Power," this banner is now in Aberdare museum.

Dai (Ropey) Penrhiwceiber, snapshot from 'All Out.'

Near the lodge there was a battered wives home and we used to feel sorry for what one girl was going through at the time, so we'd invite her in with her little baby for a cup of tea. We also had a football team and the N.C.B. had the cheek to try and buy them off by providing twelve shirts for the team. Needless to say the team would not go on the field with N.C.B. on their shirts and they burnt them.

There was help coming from all over the country and abroad. In Ireland the Dubliners remembered a boat load of food sent over to help to feed the Irish people back in 1913, when Jim Larkin was Irish Trade Unions leader. Wales sent food and supplies on that boat just before WW1 started in 1913 they were still grateful and returned the kindness.

Strike End

What ended the strike was the fact that help was starting to dwindle and life was more of a struggle. We were defeated, Scargill, Heathfield, McCarthy, we were told at the time that there would be six pits left, when in fact there was only one.

At the end of the strike, there was a very bad relationship with officials. Myself and three others had previously asked to speak with N.A.C.O.D.S and explained that we wanted to fight to keep the pit open, Joe Keepins said "It's in your interest too." We had also asked for a weekly donation for the miners, but only one person voted for it; Mike Griffin, he was our hero, Mike died 24 years ago, but he was very supportive of the miners and their families and represented them as much as he could, he could hold a great conference and spoke sense. The day we were due to return to work, we had brought the lodge banner and stretched it across the gates, unfortunately this delayed everybody's return to work, as at the sight of the banner everybody presumed we were still on strike.

Looking Back

When I was 15 years old, I started working in the pit; after working in the mine I was too tired to be hanging around on street corners. I feel sorry for the youngsters nowadays, with the lack of employment. In those days it was more difficult to replace a horse that died than a man that died. The government couldn't get out quick enough; all that's left is Glasbrook Field, The Mike Griffin Stand and The Penrhiwceiber Institute, which I am struggling to keep open. The mine was the heart of the community and the miners used to pay a weekly amount to keep Penrhiwceiber Club and library open. Things have changed so much; nothing is as it used to be. Our motto back then was 'close knit' for no matter what you did as long as the member told the truth he would be dealt with fairly.

Snapshot from 'All Out,' In 1984 the majority of Penrhiwceiber's workforce was employed by the NCB.

A lot of Welsh miners went to work on the tunnel, but they wouldn't employ the Kent boys as they were blacklisted, even though they had supported us during the strike. Locally, scabs who used to be friends have never been spoken to again.

Pamela Butts – Penrhiwceiber

Pamela was 37 at the time of the strike, she is the daughter of a miner, (her father was just ten years old when he started in the pits) the wife of a miner and a mother of three small children at the time. She was heavily involved in the women's aid group as well as attending picket lines.

Taking Action

With a husband and three small children to feed, times were hard. The men were away picketing most of the time and the women were left at home to look after the kids. It was decided in our community that us women were going to stand by our men. We would stand up and be counted, the strike wasn't just affecting the miners, but their whole families.

A meeting was held at the Penrhiwceiber Legion, it had been organised by the late Barbara Curtis. We had a good response, the women knew we had to do something to help. It was also nice to talk to other women in the same position. So the women's group was born. When we first started off we would split into groups and go from house to house asking people if they could spare some food. At first it was quite embarrassing, but you just got used to it, at the end of the day we had hungry kids to feed.

The response in our local village was excellent, even women who were not miners wives were happy to help. I think they knew how much we were struggling, however, in other areas the response was not always so good. Sometimes we were hollered at and I remember once someone let the dogs loose on us. We would collect enough food for a small parcel for every miner, every week. This would be the food that had been donated, and from people who had allotments. It wasn't a lot, but I would make sure the children were fed, even if it meant me and my husband going without.

There were clothes and food being sent from around the country and abroad. Many other groups were involved in raising money for the miners, even a free concert in Hyde Park in London.

The winter months leading up to Christmas were the worst times, I spent sleepless nights worrying about what my children would get for Christmas. The women's group had toys donated from different parts of the country and we could go and select one or two things for each of the kids. Nevertheless

Christmas in 1984 was one of the toughest Christmases ever.

This notice was pinned on the Penrhiwceiber Workingman's Hall door, below: queuing for food, snapshots from 'All Out.'

The weather was bleak, frost covered the ground and it was freezing. Me and the kids used to go over the tips and grab a few carrier bags of coal to keep us going. I remember my father had just been released from hospital, my mother was nagging him to get coal, so he put his clothes on over his pyjamas and went to get coal as me and the kids were ill. He got picked up by the police, they took him in and fined him ten shillings. My husband was always away picketing and on a few occasions came home with cuts and bruises.

Women on the Picket Line

I loved picketing, I felt I was doing something useful. We would be given a bus and a load of us women would travel the country and join the men on the picket lines. Yes, some of the miners were violent, but the sheer brutality I would see off the police was beyond belief. The women would holler abuse at the scabs when they entered the colliery's. I witnessed the police hitting miners with their truncheons, and throwing them like pieces of meat into the back of their vans. On some occasions myself and some of the other women would creep past the police and release the miners from the vans.

The police were horrible to the women, they did not want us on the picket lines. They would tell us that they were going on holiday to Spain thanks to Maggie Thatcher paying them. It was a bit harsh, when they knew we had no food, but that's what they were like. Most of them probably had wives and children themselves, but they had no compassion.

I witnessed a group of police officers being very brutal to the Greenham Common women who had sat in the middle of the road. They were picking them up and throwing them as if they were nothing. They had no respect for the miners or their wives. When we were in Port Talbot an old lady used to bring squash out for the picketers, she used to leave a key out under a flower pot for us to go the toilet as the police would follow us.

The daily newspapers and the news would be littered with pictures of miners attacking police, especially 'The Sun,' which I call 'The Scab' newspaper, to this day I will not buy it. It was very rare that you saw the pure extent of brutality that was inflicted on the miners by police reported. I had no respect for them then and still to this day I will not forget their actions.

On Thatcher

When asked about Mrs. Thatcher, Pam cannot keep the sarcasm, anger and bitterness from her voice, just hearing her name triggers pent up emotions from the past. Her face shows the suffering and there are tears in her eyes as she talks of the pain her family endured under Thatcher.

Don't get me started on her, she was afraid of the miners and their unions. They had defeated Heath and she knew she was next in line. If she had, had her way she would have flooded the whole of the South Wales Valley's with the women and children in it. She betrayed the working class people and showed no remorse in doing so. Her and Scargill had a vendetta and in my opinion Scargill used the miners to try and settle the score. If the miners had won they would have turfed her out, whereas the Conservatives ended up doing it anyway.

A couple of years ago a man was arrested for hitting the head off a statue of Thatcher, he was sent to jail, in my opinion he should have been awarded a medal.

Community Spirit

The community spirit was fabulous, we were all in the same boat and kept each other going. All the miners and their wives had a close bond even before the strike. We used to spend our miners fortnights down in Porthcawl, altogether, over the Jolly Sailor, with sandwiches and a ball for the kids. Our front doors could be left open without fear of being broken into, before and during the strike our community was very strong, close knit.

A trip was organised for the children and my three, along with many others and some adults went on a fifty two seater bus to Hastings for the weekend, the generosity of people we didn't know was overwhelming. There was also a day trip to Barry Island and Surrey sent parcels down and took some of the children up there for a week. The French, Belgians and Russians supported us with food parcels. We had help from Churches and various Lesbian and Gay groups also gave aid.

The women were the backbone of the strike, other women who's husbands worked in different trades, like building, would give us big bags of frozen food to help out. Even though nobody had much, we just put up with it and made the best of it, however some people did try and take advantage: Dirty Donna came to ask for help, she had no husband, she was on the social and she came to ask for food parcels, apparently she had spent her money on a wig.

Present Day

Nowadays it's very different, you can't leave your doors open, there are kids hanging around on street corners with nothing to do. Drugs are rife and crime is higher. If the pits were open I do not think our area would be so poverty stricken. I would do it all again with no hesitation, if it meant bringing the pits back to the Valleys. Back in the day they had reasonable wages, even though the work was dangerous, many died and there were accidents, people still went back to work and appreciated having a job to go to. It meant security for themselves and their families.

Women's Support Groups

Women played a very active part in this strike, with support groups springing up all over the country.

Photograph courtesy of National Museum – Big Pit: Blaenavon.

The following timetable taken from the book, 'Penallta,' shows a section from the diary of The Rhymney Valley Women's support group. Some could begin picketing as early as 3.40am and were at their own jobs by 8 o'clock. All this was undertaken as well as having to look after their families.

Diary Dates

MAY   21st   1st meeting to establish group

23rd   Port Talbot Women's Picket

31st   Women start to organise weekly food collections

JUNE   2nd   Caerphilly demonstration:banner appears for the 1st time

14th   Set up weekly food collection stall in Bargoed

23rd   Demonstration against Thatcher at Porthcawl

27th   Lobby of Parliament

JULY   7th   Jumble Sale - Gelligaer

14th   Save the Pits – Disco - Cascade

15th   Visit to Welbeck - Nottingham

27th   Rally in Abertillery

30th   Lobby of Welsh Office

AUG   4th   Anti Joy Watson demonstration - Aberdare

7th   Lobby of R.V.D.C. offices – re: food vouchers

11th   National Women's demonstration - London

12th   Gelligaer Fete

18th   Chartist March - Newport

29th   Labour Party trip to Barry

SEPT   2nd   Lobby of T.U.C. - Brighton

13th   Support The Miners Disco - Tredomen

27th   Collections start at Catnic

29th   Barbeque and Disco – Cefn Hengoed

30th   Eve of Conference Rally (Labour Party – Blackpool)

Women took on new responsibilities for payment of bills and other chores previously handled by the men-folk. The whole experience gave them a newfound confidence in their own ability. As a result they and their families have become more politically aware, some have embarked on further education courses to improve themselves academically.

The '84 dispute was a traumatic and distressing time for many, but it certainly had its positive aspects. Lasting friendships were made and a camaraderie engendered that will never be forgotten. Leading members of the Rhymney Valley Support Group were: Mrs. Betty Elliot, Mrs. Cath Francis, Mrs. Sonja James. (Penallta,p.65/66)

(The book Penallta was put together by Lewis Girls' Comprehensive School and printed in 1994, it won awards from; Welsh Heritage and The Prince of Wales Trust.)

A Personal History of the Miners Strike by Tim Richards

Tim lives in Abertridwr and is now retired but definitely not inactive, as a founding member of The Red Poets, now in its 19th year he regularly performs his poetry and produces yearly publications. He is also busy with many personal projects as well as writing articles for Planet-The Welsh Internationalist and Private Eye. The picture below shows Tim and the Rhymney Valley Miners Support Group during the strike, Tim is in the front row second man from the left.

The Miners Strike of 1984-85 was a turning point in the history of Wales as the defeat of the miners marked the end of an era in our economy, society and politics. It might seem presumptuous for me, a further education college law lecturer to write a personal history of the strike but I was there and became deeply involved, so while this is not a definitive history I can at least tell the story as I experienced it.

When the strike started in March 1984, I volunteered to help giving free legal advice. I advised some South Wales miners arrested for giving out leaflets against scabs in Nottingham and as the police were still finding their way about the law, they originally charged them with giving out obscene publications! I joke not – that is how the police worked from start to finish – arrest first and find reasons later.

The 1972 and 1974 miners strikes had taught the Tories and the miners the same lesson – starve the country of coal and the miners would win but the Tories were better prepared. When the miners on strike found that they could get no benefits and that the union had no money to help them they faced starvation and rapid defeat before they even started.

Unfortunately, in April 1984, this was only just being fully realised by the South Wales NUM.

It was while I was giving legal advice in their Pontypridd HQ that Kim Howells, their researcher, explained the desperate need for support groups to feed the miners' families and that is how I came to set up the Rhymney Valley Miners Support Group (RVMSG) As a political activist who had helped the Nantgarw Coking Ovens NUM lodge in their campaign against its closure by Labour in 1978 and had addressed NUM lodges on the threat posed by Thatcher's nuclear power programme before the strike, I had contacts and called the first meeting in Caerphilly Workmen's Hall.

It was one of the first miners support groups to get organised and it was one of the largest as it covered the NUM lodges of Nantgarw/ Windsor and Nantgarw Coking ovens, Caerphilly tar plant, Bedwas and Penallta. Because we were ahead of the South Wales NUM we did not fit their plans so we were added, arbitrarily, to the Gwent Food fund, even though we were largely outside Gwent. It took the media a while to catch up too and at our third meeting a BBC news team turned up to film it and I agreed but only if they paid us. I am still awaiting the cheque.

Early on in the strike we got hold of a newsletter produced by the Dulais Valley Miners Support Group and we decide to produce our own weekly newsletter "Rhymney Valley Report" which had a print run of 3 - 4,000 and was distributed outside the valley because there was nothing else in our area. As the support for the miners grew, one of the earliest developments was the local Miners Wives Support Groups that sprung up and which we supported as they developed into wider activities beyond food collection and distribution to joining the picket lines.

My whole life outside work revolved around the strike. We held meetings on Sundays, either in Penyrheol or Bedwas, and I would then type up our weekly newsletter, the Rhymney Valley Report (RVR) on my BBC B computer, print it on a dot matrix printer, add pictures and written headlines and hand it over to Lyn the printer in the Rhymney Valley District Council (RVDC) where I would pick it up on a Wednesday for distribution on Thursdays.

Then I was out collecting food and money over the weekend in the streets and going round the houses. In my village of Abertridwr, as throughout the South Wales valleys, the response to our collections was overwhelmingly supportive even though the number of miners actually working was tiny in comparison to the population. Some memories remain vivid – like the time I called on a young couple with a baby in a rather bare terraced house near where I lived. They invited me into a largely empty kitchen with no food around then rummaged in their cupboard to find some tins of food for us. I felt humbled by their spirit of support and if the miners could have survived on that alone then they would still be out on strike today.

We began the summer with a demonstration, organising marches from Abertridwr, Ystrad Mynach and Bedwas, (representing the local NUM lodges) to Caerffili where they joined to march round the town to Morgan Jones Park for a public meeting. We managed to co-ordinate the marches meeting up, by having leaders of each march in touch with me, on the Abertridwr march, using local CB enthusiasts. It took a lot of organising to get it right but I was as pleased as punch when they all met up smoothly at the Piccadilly crossroads.

Politics in the area was dominated by Labour and Plaid Cymru and their active members support was crucial. I believe that being a Welsh socialist in neither party explains why I was chosen to be Chairperson and helped me to chair meetings in a fair way that was acceptable to both sides.

Being a large group had its advantages, as when, in the Summer of 1984, George Melly offered to do some fund-raising concerts. We hosted one of them in the Aneurin Labour club in Penyrheol and this was one of the strike's high moments. When George Melly did his concert he introduced himself by saying; "'DIS OLE STRIKE'S GONNA GET IT SOME STYLE". He was living in Brecon and his wife Diane organised his mini-tour and George loved the audience of miners and their families as much as they loved him. It was at this concert that I first heard the newly-formed Côr Cochion Caerdydd, the Cardiff Red Choir, which is still going.

But, when it came to the Karl Francis film "Ms. Rhymney Valley 1985" the experience was less positive as the film created tensions within the group and I remember wondering why he had not even approached his local miners support group while making the film. The film was alright in itself but it had nothing to say about the strike and lacked something because of it. I am afraid that when I saw it the only thing I noticed was the scene where Neil Kinnock entered a club in Bedwas and the audience appeared to welcome him. In fact, it was the only scene where I was around when they filmed it and in my recollection the response was negative amongst many miners in the room and he was actually booed.

One aspect of the miners strike which has been swept from the pages of history - is the lack of support from Labour MPs and how it was seen by the miners. We were so unimpressed with Ron Davies we invited him to a meeting to explain why he had not bothered to turn up to a Public Meeting we organised in January 1985. His absence and the attendance of Plaid Cymru MP Dafydd Ellis Thomas was contrasted by many miners with the lukewarm support of local Labour MPs.

One of the high points of the strike for me happened at a fund-raising event in Pontlottyn when I was introduced to Will Paynter, the legendary NUM and Communist leader who was

81, but, looked, walked, talked and thought 20 years younger.

Miners of his generation had fought the battles of the General

Strike and the 1930s and it was a battle repeated during 1984 /

85 when the miners once again faced the full aggressive power

of the British state represented by the police who had learnt the

lessons of the flying pickets of the 1972 and 1974 strikes.

But it was the experience of Orgreave that really taught

the miners what they were facing – the raw force of the new

paramilitary tactics developed by the police. Their suspicions

were aroused when they got there as instead of being

obstructive the police actually told them where to park. As one

miner told me "There was no doubt about it – it was an exercise

aimed at giving us a real pasting". This was a view supported

years later by ex-Chief Constable Alderson, of Devon and

Cornwall in a documentary about Orgreave. Looking at the

police's own video he concluded that the trouble was actually

started by the police. Nothing has changed as similar

aggression was used by the police in the Climate Change demo

a few years ago. Another similarity was the fact that many

police officers during the miners strike displayed no badge

numbers, which, of course, makes them more difficult to identify. The miners were capable of direct action themselves, I well remember a couple of our group who were in high spirits at one meeting, they had managed to sabotage a train load of coal by opening the doors on the railway trucks to pour the loads onto the line.

As the strike wore on, the issue of scabbing became important as other areas, like North Wales, drifted back to work and became scabs, tempted by a bonus bribe from the NCB. Our response was to increase the venom we poured on them and several issues of the weekly newsletter concentrated on this, with cartoons such as the "Anatomy of a Scab" with an explanation of his gormless head - "Eyes – can't see what he is doing. Nose – can't smell himself. Ears – listens to what he wants to hear. Mouth – always open, giving excuses. Brain – the only part not working."

It was in this climate of frustration and anger that the miners reacted to the first scabbing in South Wales and this led to the tragic killing of a Cardiff taxi driver David Wilkie, on the Heads of the Valley road near Rhymney in December 1984 when two miners Dean Hancock and Russell Shankland dropped a concrete block into the path of a taxi taking a scab to work. When they were convicted of murder the reaction in the valley was shock as we believed that they had not intended to kill anyone and that became the key issue in the case which was finally resolved long after the strike had finished. When the House of Lords dismissed the murder charge, they replaced it with manslaughter and issued guidelines for future juries in a sensible and clear precedent which asks a jury to assess first the likelihood of an act leading to death and then consider whether, as a result, it might have been foreseen and therefore intended.

When we had to go out collecting soon after the accident, we were not sure how people would react, but, we should not have worried and the Christmas spirit lifted us when we went carol singing. It was a hard time and one episode is particularly telling. Some miners had seen what the Gwent Food Fund had planned for the meagre Christmas meal and not unreasonably they argued that the RVMSG had raised large sums of money while other areas were not as well-organised and that we should keep back some of the cash we had raised to buy something extra for our local families. After a heated debate it was decided that we should not do that as everyone should get the same. Although no-one said it, this was a practical application of the Marx's principle for Communism, "From each according to their ability, to each according to their needs."

The miners' political consciousness was broad and it was no surprise to me that a number of them joined an anti-nuclear power demonstration at Hinkley Point in Somerset one weekend despite the fact that they got no travel expenses. On the other hand, those politics also engendered wonderful camaraderie as we supported a group of isolated striking miners in Nottinghamshire who were ostracised by their local community of scabs in a mirror image of our experience. The stresses and strains of staying out on strike created huge problems and tensions in marriages which inevitably led, sometimes, to bitterness and divorce and the children of the miners were often damaged too.

The South Wales miners had been slow in joining the strike partly because of resentment that they had not been supported in their call for support against pit closures in the valleys in late 1983. It was a considered and realistic view of many South Wales miners that the strike had come too late, that starting a strike in March was stupid because the demand for coal dropped after the winter and it would take longer to starve the country of coal. But when the strike started in earnest, South Wales joined with a vengeance and maintained a 99% turnout, more than any other area, until it finished.

The end of the strike came fast and the straw that broke the camel's back happened when Kim Howells spoke to the Media about the return to work. Why a lowly, unelected researcher for the South Wales NUM was the main spokesman was, and still is, a mystery, but many of us noted his rapid elevation to become Labour MP for Pontypridd and the questions remain, 30 years on.

As Arthur Scargill had predicted, and we had always known would happen, Margaret Thatcher then closed down the coal-mining industry including a handful of pits in South Wales which were still profitable, the proof of which was evidenced by the success of Tower colliery for a decade after. But revenge was not long in coming as the Anti-Poll Tax campaign of the early 90's saw many of the same people fighting back and winning, but that is another story. (Planet, 197. p.p 30/35)

Tim's poem first appeared in The Red Poets Issue 5

The Dark Valley

It was a silent night,
its darkness disturbed
by the low throaty
roar of an underground fan.

In that quiet night,
the Windsor mine breathed
and the ventilation shaft
exhumed stank air from the pit.

In the dark, silent void,
The slow persistent sound
of that fan continued,
breathing life.

In that night
of struggle, the depths
exhaled resistance,
a future gasping for air.

In that desperate night,
I dreamed of failure,
of bitter death
and suffocation.

In that dark night,
they killed us,
turned out the light,
destroyed our rights.

Tonight, I listen,
ten years on,
and nothing breathes.
The mine is dead.

But, in the middle of the night,
I remember the dark roar
when the ground beneath us breathed
and we fought for life.

*Pickets and Police at Nantgarw- top,Tonypandy Miners – bottom,
photographs courtesy of National Museum Wales – Big Pit:Blaenavon.*

Ceri Thompson - Curator of Big Pit National Coal Museum in Blaenavon.

Ceri was born in The Rhondda Valley in 1953. His family has a history of mining going back to the early 19th Century in the Risca area. His grandfather started working for the mines at the age of eleven, but in those days wasn't allowed underground until he turned twelve.

Photograph courtesy of National Museum, Big Pit: Blaenavon. Striking at Aberthaw Power Station, Ceri is the one on the left.

In 1972 the strikes had been won after causing the lights to go out, following that the 1974 strike which was monetary was also won. For a while afterwards it went reasonably quiet, until 1979, the Thatcher era. She didn't want to pour money into so called 'lost industries.' When she was elected we realised we were in for a fight. Thatcher's government were already preparing, buying land to keep coal stocks on and debating whether or not to use the army to move coal.

In 1983 there was an overtime ban on and money was already short, on a Monday morning we'd have to wait for security checks, it was not ideal. In March 1984 there was a small motion of votes to come out on strike. On the Monday morning my buddy George was on the picket line from Maerdy. By the Wednesday there was a new lodge meeting called, after that we came out to support Maerdy and I signed up for picketing. Me and George were inseparable during the strike, mostly we were at Aberthaw power station, but when we went up to South Derbyshire, the amount of police presence there shocked me, there was a phalanx of police, twenty deep, marching towards the pickets.

A lot of the pubs and shops refused to serve us, because many of the mines in that area were still working. We stayed at the Community centre and got fed with the O.A.P.'s. At first we were under the impression that we could talk on the picket lines, however, we discovered that normally that was not allowed. Things became uncomfortable, very pushy and shovy. Orgreave tactics were to block mass picketing, there were many arrests in Nottingham and the N.U.M. had injunctions taken out against them.

Sometimes we went rabbiting and 'borrowing' from farmers fields to get some extra food. The Nottingham area was more of a farming area with a history of scabbing. My uncle was a Methodist Minister in Nottingham and en route to his parish he was stopped by the police, they wouldn't believe he wasn't a miner just because of his Welsh accent.

In the autumn we picketed outside Cwm, there wasn't any trouble except there were a few hairy moments with the Gwent police. The South Wales N.U.M. was the strongest area in Britain. Eventually the N.U.M. thought it was better to all go back together, rather than have a civil war, but we still tried to fight to get the sacked men their jobs back. I'm still surprised that so many people stayed out as long as they did, it was such a harrowing time, but we did get to go to a lot of places that we wouldn't have gone otherwise, such as the Brighton T.U.C.

conference.

Even though the 5 a.m. starts were hard, when the pit doors closed many of us were lost. I started working at Cwm Colliery at the age of sixteen, even though my parents didn't want me to go underground. I worked on the coalface for sixteen years until Cwm Colliery closed in 1986. After that I didn't want to go anywhere else, nothing seemed safe. It was really hard for the men to find jobs. I tried many times and was told only women were wanted.

The generosity and support we received enabled us to stay out as long as we did. My wife was fully supportive throughout the strike. When we returned it was really difficult, faces had closed up under pressure. It was hard work trying to make the faces workable again, once I fell asleep. The reviews in November of 1986 included Nantgarw and Cwm, usually one of the reviewed pits was destined for closure. This time however, for the first time, the decision was made to close the two pits. My grandfather also died that same day. It was like the end of an era.

Whilst on the picket lines I had started to learn Welsh, so I began going to Clwb –Y – Bont to take lessons. I met the M.P. Wayne David whilst there and he suggested that I go to Coleg Harlech. He sent me a booklet and I went to Coleg Harlech and studied Welsh Literature and Welsh History, mostly industrial, from there I went to Cardiff University. Education had been important to the N.U.M. with people like Kim Howells and Dai Francis, who were trying to lead people to a brighter future.

I now help to keep the Mining heritage alive at Big Pit Museum, Blaenafon. I also publish 'The Glo Coal' magazine, telling personal and historical stories of the Mining Industry. The magazines are available on Big Pit website and at Big Pit Museum itself. As part of the National Museum of Wales, Big Pit is free to visit and is a great day out for families, also giving you the chance to go down a real mine.

The Flying Pickets

Brian Hibbard yn Big Pit, 2008
Brian Hibbard at Big Pit in 2008

The late Brian Hibbard was interviewed by Ceri Thompson - National Museum, Big Pit in 2009 for the Glo Coal publication 'Strike,' commemorating 25 years since the 1984/85 strike. Ceri kindly agreed to let us use the interview. It shows instances of generosity from the entertainment industry in force.

I was born in Ebbw Vale, my grandfather was a miner. I had the option of going down the pit or into Ebbw Vale Steel Works when I left school – so I went into the steelworks. I suppose I have always been a socialist and my first jobs in acting were in political theatre companies. We actually did a show about the 1972 Housing Finance Act, which we toured for a year and sold out. I later joined a theatre company called '7:84' which stood for '7% of the population control 84% of the wealth.' I joined them to do a show called *'One Big Blow'* which was about a miners' brass band. It was incredibly successful and we did two tours of the South Wales Valleys. We'd have a couple of pints after, and then we'd all jump into the back of the transit van and start singing for our own amusement.

There was a community theatre in Deptford asking if I could get the boys to sing in a benefit concert. We debated what we were going to call ourselves. Because of our involvement in the 1972 and 1974 miners' strike up in Yorkshire, we decided to cll ourselves 'The Flying Pickets.' We did a show celebrating The Peasants Revolt with Tony Benn and after did a lot of benefits (as a kind of hobby) until 'The Flying Pickets' really took off. We knew that there was a demand for 'The Flying Pickets,' your talking now about the early years of Thatcherism, and there was an obvious movement against her, you know, "Against the bitch!" So we did lots of gigs – we did a cabaret circuit with people like Alexei Sayle, Ben Elton, Rick Mayall, bald Keith Alllen – all that gang; and that was incredibly successful. We ended up doing tours, very large tours, with people like Dionne Warwick and then we had the number one hit record, *'Only You.'* We had all been involved in political theatre for years and then to suddenly find ourselves on *'Top of The Pops,'* thinking f*****g hell, whose idea was this boys?

When the miners went on strike, I was immediately on the phone to the NUM offices saying "What do you want us to do?" So the three of us ended up going to Drax Power Station and standing on the picket line there and it gor national coverage. The record company Virgin weren't happy with us and told us we couldn't go. So we said; "What are you going to do then, have a picket line at Kings Cross Station to stop us jumping on the train to Yorkshire?" Then the second single came out called *'When Your Young and in Love.'* I was amazed at the reactions when we went on television promoting the single and said that we supported the miners.

God, W.H.Smith wouldn't stock the album because of our associations with 'thuggery!' People like Henry Kelly and Harry Carpenter would make jibes at us on television. I suppose career-wise it was probably detrimental. But that wasn't the point, we were political animals and we had to go the way we did.

I lived in south-east London at the time and I was walking around The Cutty Sark in Greenwich one night and met some boys from Bettws pit, Ammanford. They were looking for somewhere to stay so we gave them the key to the flat. They used to use it as a base to come up collecting. I think they were surprised by the reception they got in south-east London as they were welcomed with open arms. In a lot of pubs they didn't have to buy a pint. We did gigs for the NUM in Kent, we did a benefit in The Albert Hall with Dennis Skinner, Alexei Sayle and the reggae band Azwad, we did what we could to support the miners.

They were organising a raffle for the NUM in Ebbw Vale, so they asked me if there was anything I could raffle. I said "Yes, you can have one of the donkey jackets with 'The Flying

Pickets' on the back." I was in Birmingham at the time doing a show and I had to get this donkey jacket down to Ebbw Vale. I hitched down – and I've never got there so quickly! We'd had the hit record and I was quite distinctive with the side burns and I was standing beside the road and all of a sudden this car comes to a halt and the driver says; "f*****g hell mate, I just had you on the radio, where you going?" I said "I'm taking a donkey jacket down to Ebbw Vale" and I got to Ebbw Vale and back in about four hours – just to drop a donkey jacket to raise money for the miners!

I think that Thatcher engineered the confrontation with Scargill and 'militarised' the police force throughout the early part of her 'reign.' They practised in the Brixton and Handsworth riots of 1981. I remember those boys going up to Orgreave and being just blown away by the violence of the police against unarmed miners just fighting for their jobs. I think that Thatcher was determined that what happened to the Heath Government in 1974 was never going to happen again. When she said that there was no such thing as society, what she really wanted to say was there was no such thing as working class communities.

The defeat of the miners completely destroyed the trade union movement in this country but Thatcher also succeeded in creating the 'me – generation.' She created the property – owning democracy, she sold off council houses. I mean, how do kids who were brought up in a council house, doing manual jobs get on the housing ladder? I was working in London and you'd see the people waiting for the all night bus in Trafalgar Square and they would be swigging from bottles of champagne. They had, to quote Macmillan, 'never had it so good.' It was the 'me, my money and f*** you lot!' generation, which I despised then and still do.

Image courtesy of Museum Wales, Big Pit: Blaenavon.

Siàn Morgan

Siàn lives in Blackwood with her son, she writes poetry and has recently finished her first novel after being given a bursary from Literature Wales in 2012. Siàn graduated from The University of Glamorgan with a creative and professional writing B.A. Honours. She is an activist and a conservationist.

I was fourteen when the strike started and 1984, and fifteen when it ended. The experience brought out the little protester in me. I love the motto, 'if you don't stand for something, you'll fall for anything.' I could probably write a book about the social and psychological implications, but I'm not that brainy. But I am quite proud of the fact, that my first ever gig was an Arthur Scargill concert. It wasn't really a concert, but everyone was packed in and cheering, so it felt like one at the time. I'd stood on my chair to get a better view of Scargill and MacGregor thrashing it out. Later that evening, I made an appearance on News at Ten because I happened to be in front of their camera. I was the talk of the school the next day. I'd pretended not to hear when the rude camera man kept shouting, 'Excuse me love, get out of the bloody way!' My father had told me I didn't have to move for the media,   so I stayed put.

75

The opposition, MacGregor, was at the microphone telling us why pit closures had to happen. Suddenly, no one was listening or booing because the crowd went into a joyous uproar, even the camera man's snobby English accent was drowned out. Everyone started to laugh and chant miner's anthems, 'Arthur Scargill, Arthur Scargill, we'll support you evermore.' At the time I'd been poking my tongue out at the camera, but I turned around to watch a hang-man's noose being slowly lowered from the rafters. It stopped right in front of MacGregor's face. He was not a happy man. No one wanted to hear him spouting shit with his American accent anyway. Scargill covered his face and tried to remain dignified, he was a leader after all. The jokers could be seen sitting in the rafters, giggling with mischievous camaraderie. The next day, The Sun newspaper told Britain how the evil miners had tried to hang MacGregor. My father said he would never buy 'that scab newspaper' ever again.

Months later, life for British miners and their families had become unbearable. My poor father's eyes looked deader with each passing month. That never ending struggle ruined his spirit. His family had been picked up and thrown in the gutter, along with everyone else who refused to believe Thatcher's lies. Winter came to devastate us. We had no money or coal, we were starved and frozen into submission. I remember how awful it was to be on the losing side.

The glass had cracked and fallen off our Parkray fire. My mother tried to patch the cracked pieces together with tin foil, but smoke still bellowed out and into our sitting room. The walls were blackened and the room tasted acrid. Our family and house were in a state of disrepair. Many things were broken and not replaced.

My father was never arrested on the picket line, but the police arrested him for collecting fire-wood down by the old mill. They released him without charge, because the trees had already been felled to make way for the bypass that would soon cut through our village. He told the police officers that he would be going back for more, because he would not see his children freeze to death. I was really proud of him. One day, he came home from picketing with a bad truncheon gash on the side of his head and a black eye. The police had beaten lots of others as well. So he lost faith in law and order. I was worried for him. He'd served in the Army before coming home to be a miner. He'd fought for his country in Ireland and witnessed his friend being mortally wounded. But the Government he'd fought for turned against him. I felt sorry for him. Now, much like the Irish, Africans, Indians and Aborigines, the list goes on, he also knew what it was like to have no respect and a deep resentment for the British Authorities. He just wanted his job, he wanted to be able to support his wife and three girls, I felt part of my heart break for him.

As I watched that dreadful year unfold, my contempt for the 'Authorities' grew. The government had initiated their propaganda machine with military precision. I started to believe that people in power were essentially dictators, who had no qualms about pushing people into degradation and madness. They had the media, police and an army to back them up if anyone dared to push back. I saw them as demons in disguise, they resembled people, but there was nothing human about them. No humanity, no compassion, no idea what life was like for real humans. I watched as the filthy rich got dirtier each passing day. Civilised society was a great big stinking lie because our Government were basically savages, who were never inclined to put 'women and children first.'

Looking back it was a momentous experience. Thanks to my father and the N.U.M. my eye's were opened to overcoming adverse conditions at a young age. Thanks to the Government I became 'anti-authority.' Even though I felt like a pathetic pawn, I adapted to my environment and chose to use anger-energy to fuel my will to survive. People didn't physically die but a lot of them died somewhere inside, which was far worse.

Michael Phillips

Michael Phillips from Bedlinog was also a child in the miners strike. His Father worked at the Trelewis drift in the South Wales valleys.

I was fifteen when the strike started, still in school. I remember our bus route used to take us past Merthyr Vale colliery which was being picketed at the time, the road would be littered with police and miners who would stop their scuffles and part to allow the bus through. I recall filling my pockets with stones or anything I could find and throw them out of the window of the bus at the police while passing, how I was never arrested I will never know.

Times were tough though, I was old enough to realise my family were struggling and yet still too young too help financially, food was scarce and if it was not for my grandparents and other immediate family I honestly do not know how we would have survived the strike. I had free school meals and my family would receive a food parcel which proved a lifeline to us and thousands of other needy families. 'Do you know where a lot of that food came from?' It came from Sikh and Indian communities who wanted to help the miners, people do not realise this but there was tremendous support from them. People talk about racism but there was certainly none then, the Sikhs, Indians and also the Russian miners were a great support and their kindness was greatly received by the welsh miners and their families.

I would try to help as much as I could, I would go with my Father to the local tip to collect coal. I would also do errands for my elderly neighbours who would pay me 50p for my troubles, although I had my suspicions that the elderly neighbours didn't really need the odd jobs, it was their little way of helping out. I also had a paper round and a milk round I would have to get up at 5am to start the milk round and call in to the newsagents halfway through to collect the papers to deliver before I finally got to school. I didn't mind as I would get paid £13.50 for both, it was extra booze money for me. The pubs we went to knew we were underage but couldn't really afford to send us away, we would be there for hours playing pool with a pint of Albright. I also did not have to ask my parents for anything it made me feel more independent.

My Sister got married during the strike and we had to sell our touring caravan to pay for the wedding, we had owned our little caravan for years and had spent many happy times holidaying with other mining families, our holidays were no more and I was heartbroken. Community spirit was excellent, everybody stood united, nobody had two pennies to rub together but still we all kept each other going through the tough times.

Scargill could have won that strike if only everyone had believed in him, every statement he made proved to be absolutely true. Scargill was a militant bastard mind, perhaps a bit too militant but definitely cleverer than Thatcher. However Thatcher had the police on her side, she wanted revenge on the miners for the defeat of Edward Heath, she wanted to destroy the NUM and pull other unions into line. Thatcher made this her personal vendetta and used the police and the media to win her war. Some people are under the impression that Scargill made millions out of the miners, personally I do not agree with this. I view Scargill as a man who fought courageously for the working class, for people like us. However I do think Arthur Scargill made a fatal mistake of not taking a ballot. If Scargill had taken a ballot I have no doubt in my mind we would have won that strike.

Even after all the hardship and poverty that 1984 inflicted upon our family, I still decided to pursue a career in mining. I always knew I would become a miner, it was in my blood, as a child I would play around the pits. I was also a regular visitor to Taff Colliery where my Nan worked as a kitchen assistant. I only ever read two books in my teens and both involved mining. I remember a conversation between me and my friend; we must have only been about 12 at the time. My friend wanted to go places, a good education and a high ranked job. I shrugged my shoulders and said; 'I want to go underground be a miner.'

I began my career in 1986 at Taff Colliery after a huge recruitment drive. I started off on top pit after they noticed on my application form that I had good handwriting, little did they know my Mother had kindly filled in the form for me and my handwriting was bloody awful. There was only one place I wanted to be though, underground, it was my passion and I nagged at the bosses for weeks to allow me to do so, my persistence paid off and finally I was where I had dreamed of being as a boy of 12, underground.

The atmosphere underground was good considering what the men had been through in 1984, everyone looked out for each other just as they did in the strike, you know the saying, 'you wash my back and I'll wash yours,' well that's exactly what it was like and I am sure we probably did wash each others backs in the showers. Not only did I work with these men, I socialised with them too, playing rugby and having a pint, me and my one colleague was so close they nicknamed us Urk and Burk. I had an accident underground when a roof collapsed on me and I received several cuts to my head. The men were fantastic making sure I was ok and helping me to the top of the pit and for that I will be forever grateful.

We only had one scab in Taff, technically he didn't break the strike and go back to work but he had been overheard contemplating it. He became known as half a scab and wasn't very popular with the other miners. In another pit which I won't name there was another scab who had worked all through the strike, the other miners hated him, this resulted in excrement being placed in his lunch box and his water bottle being urinated in. It was like that for all of the scabs in every pit in the valleys they were Thatcher's boys, somebody that couldn't be trusted after all they had helped her win the strike. Still to this day there is animosity towards the men who broke the strike, families were torn because of it and the scars were never healed. The motto is, 'once a scab always a scab.'

I worked in Taff for seven years before it sadly closed in 1993, there was no need for it to close, there was plenty of coal in Taff. Before the General Election they had opened up a new heading that was to go into Gelligaer, unfortunately Labour were yet again defeated by the conservatives and the very next day drams were seen full of concrete block filling up the heading. I knew then that my career as a miner was coming to an end. We were told that Taff was uneconomically viable, yet they had purchased two FSV buses worth a million pound, built new offices and concreted the top of the pit. Money was being wasted, the pit had served his purpose for over 100 years, why change things now? It was too late, an end of an era had come, coal mining in the valleys would be no more.

Things are so different now, yes the valleys are greener and the air is cleaner but without the pits the valleys are nothing, it may look nicer but that doesn't put money in our pockets. The valleys have suffered, there were sixteen shops in Bedlinog, however through the years the majority of them have beenforced to close resulting in just four shops left. Public houses are boarded up, they thrived when the mines were open with the miners calling in for an after work pint or to attend their NUM meetings. Unions are nowhere near as strong now, in every job I have been employed in since 1993 the unions have been weak and afraid to stand up for the people, they are most likely afraid of the consequences, afraid they will be dished with the same treatment as the miners.

It's a shame Britain wasn't a bit more like France they are not afraid to stand up to the Government, in France they all stand together, we will never have that in Britain again. Wages were higher in the mines. I was fetching home more in 1988 than I am now, much better wages than the factories today.

I would go back down the mines tomorrow if I was given the opportunity. Although, health and safety would never allow it now. Back then there were no toilets and we would eat our lunch without washing our hands and sit wherever we could, usually on a plank of wood. I miss the mines and I am still haunted by the sounds of the skip winder and the metal plate beneath my feet as I stepped off the cage. The distinct smell of the coal dust and the overpowering smell of the soap we used to wash with is still with me and the sight of the miners eyes that looked like they had been wearing eye liner. I believe coal will return to the valleys one day but in the form of open cast mining, which in my opinion just doesn't look as natural as the mines we love and miss in the valleys.

Natalie Butts-Thompson

Natalie lives in Penrhiwceiber with her husband and two daughters, she is a 2nd year History and English student at The University of South Wales, her eldest daughter Sophie also attends the same university. The mining history is close to her own heart as both her father and grandfather were miners. She co-produced this book as part of this years work placement project.

Coal In The Snow – Photograph courtesy of Gayle O' Dare – Cynon Valley Remembered. Natalie is second from the right)

I was just nine at the time of the miners strike but it is

something I will never forget, some of my memories are good

some not so good. The people of Penrhiwceiber, my little

village, were like one big family during the strike; after all, most of us were in the same position so I never felt different to any of the other kids. We didn't have the latest clothes or toys but we always made our own fun, collecting newspapers and stones and pretending to be a fish shop or playing hopscotch.

I can recall sneaking over the Cwm Cynon tip with my brother and his friends to steal coal, I was never asked to by my parents but I felt I was helping out. The tip would be littered with people, men, women and some children all with their nylon sacks and shopping baskets collecting coal for their family. I remember being there once with half a sack of coal when the police arrived, I ran towards the bridge got half way across and my skirt fell down to my ankles I do not know if it was a hand me down from my elder sister or if I was losing weight but either way I ran the rest of the way home holding my skirt up with one hand and dragging the sack with the other, needless to say there was not much coal left in the sack by the time I reached home.

I cannot recall going hungry during the strike, however I do remember meals being repetitive, beans on toast or sardines on toast (which I hated and still do to this day, but still

Managed to eat) or on a good day we would have stew if we were lucky enough to get corned beef in our parcel. We would also get a meal on a Saturday at Penrhiwceiber School; all the miners would be there.

Although I was only a child at the time I could sense my parents were struggling to make ends meet and I suspect they often went hungry to feed us children. I used to worry all the time when my parents were out picketing and instead of watching grange hill or blue peter I would be glued to the Welsh news, anxious to catch a glimpse of my parents and see that they were alright. I remember spotting my Dad in a confrontation with the police, I think it was at the phurnacite plant in Fernhill, there were about seven police officers laying into my dad and other miners trying to help him, I was really upset at seeing this and from that day lost all respect for the police. My Father would often come home battered and bruised but he would just dust himself down and get ready for the next day, this is where my respect lies with my Dad and the rest of the miners who fought daily for what they believed in.

We also must not forget the Women, Tammy Wynette

must have written her song about them, 'stand by your man,' because that is exactly what they did. In our village the Women were fantastic, arranging food parcels, collecting money and even arranging day trips as a treat for the children, some even ventured from the village for the first time and joined their men on the picket line.

I remember the woman organising a day trip to Barry Butlin's, there was so much excitement amongst us children we had been looking forward to it for a while, I believe around three buses left Penrhiwceiber that morning full of smiling happy children, we had a fantastic day.

I was also lucky enough to spend some time away in Surrey and Hastings again arranged by the Women's group, I recall being very nervous about leaving my family to stay with strangers but I needn't have been as the families were kind and loving people who treated us really well. I cannot recall the name of the family in Surrey but I do remember the name of the Hastings family; the Browns, Maureen, Anita and Anthony and to them I would like to say a huge thank you for their kindness in 1984.

Christmas time was the hardest, the weather was bleak and I knew my family were struggling to keep the house warm, baths were limited as we needed coal for hot water. I remember lying in bed Christmas eve worrying, I was nine now and did not believe in Father Christmas any more but I wished there was one.

I wished just for one present to open on Christmas morning, I had not asked my parents for anything as I knew money was tight. My wish came true because in the morning I awoke to not just one present but quite a few more than I had imagined. Maybe Father Christmas had been unable to work his magic but the women's group most certainly had worked theirs, collecting toys and food parcels for weeks to ensure that every mining family had a magical Christmas and thanks to them we most certainly did. So the title of Iron Lady in my opinion goes to the thousands of women who stood by their men throughout the hardest battle of their lives, the miner's wives.

I am proud to come from a mining family and proud to say we were part of the 1984 miners strike. Community spirit has died since then and due to Thatcher and the Tory Government little villages like mine have been ruined. Thatcher betrayed the working classes took away their jobs and ripped the hearts out of their communities but one thing she could not take away from them was their dignity and pride.

Kids In Coal:Photograph courtesy of Gayle O'Dare: Cynon Valley Remembered.

Looking for Coal. Photograph courtesy of Gayle O' Dare: Cynon Valley Remembered.

Coal not Hole

It was a cold Saturday morning, I was snuggled up on the sofa with my brother watching my favourite programme, top of the pops, my sister was sitting on the floor in the corner of the room listening to her new record of Adam and the Ants and giggling annoyingly with her best friend Julie.

I turned back to my programme and turned up the volume to drown out the noise, as I did, my programme vanished and instead a man with a bright multicoloured jumper and glasses too big for his face appeared, standing by a map with a serious expression, "weather warning for South Wales," he announced in a concerned voice "heavy snow will hit South Wales tonight and may last for several weeks," he continued. The room was silent now, all eyes were on the telly, I looked at my brother who was staring in horror, he started to rub his nose he always did that when he was worried or in trouble. I knew why he was worried, it was November of 1984.

The whole of the mining villages in the South Wales valleys were out on strike, had been since March, coal was running low now and everyone relied on it for heat and hot water. "I have to go and get coal" my brother shouted, my father usually went but he was away today picketing, he was always away lately, I missed him. My mum was out too, collecting parcels of food with the miners wives, I normally went with her but it was too cold today she had said and I had been left under the watchful eye of the dreaded sister who was now speaking, "Well I'm not going its waay too cold," her friend Julie sat beside her nodding her head in agreement.

"I'll come" I blurted out almost before I thought it, "I want to, I'm not staying with her," I said; pointing to where my sister was sat.

"Ok but wrap up warm squirt" replied my brother giving my head an affectionate pat, "well go call for Dai then he will help us".

Ten minutes later I was ready, wearing so many layers of clothes I could hardly move my arms and a hat so big you could hardly see my eyes, we were ready to go; joined by Dai we made the short journey across the road and over the bridge to the old coal tip.

The tip was huge a sea of black, there were quite a few people here already, men and women, you could see them in the distance jumping in and out of holes with their shovels filling their nylon sacks with coal. Once full they would carry the sacks on their back or transport them in old prams to safety, in fear of the police arriving and taking the bags. You see what we were doing was illegal, theft in fact but everyone was desperate for heat and prepared to go to any lengths to keep themselves and their family warm.

Mr. Jones an elderly plump man called out to us when he saw us approach "howbe kids, your old man out picketing is he?"

"Yeah butt" answered my brother pushing his shovel into the hard ground, "in that case tell your mother I'll pop in two bags later butt" said Mr. Jones, he was like that was Mr. Jones, very kind, so was everyone else though the community spirit was very much alive.

My brother handed me a griddle as him and Dai shovelled for coal "put the coal through here and shake it" he said gesturing towards the coal. I did as I was told shaking the coal and filling the nylon bags then dragging them to a hiding place, the bags were heavy, I was cold now too, my face was stinging and my nose was running, the coal dust clogged in my chest and made me cough and splutter but I kept filling the bags, listening to the conversation between my brother, Dai and Mr. Jones.

I felt grown up listening to their comments about the police, 'pigs' they called them, I laughed along with them when they referred to the miners who worked as scabs and secretly enjoyed hearing their foul language. All of a sudden there was a loud screech of tyres, women and men picked up their sacks and scattered towards the bridge, men in black uniforms charged out of the white vans, it was the police, "hide" shouted my brother and Dai, Mr. Jones had vanished. I looked around, it was like something out of a battleground, men were fighting with the police and women were screaming obscenities at them as they ripped open the sacks of coal "fucking pig" shouted one woman before running off.

"Hide," shouted my brother frantically as he ran off, I looked around me in complete panic, I was so scared now I could hardly breathe, I could feel my knees knocking together, I jumped into the hole where Mr Jones had been digging. I sat there quietly my knees bent up into my chest, my teeth were chattering from the cold and fright. I looked around me, the hole was quite big, Mr. Jones must have been digging for hours I thought to myself, the hole was very deep but not very wide I examined the coal that stared me right in the face and scraped it with my fingernail it felt hard and cold and was glistening, like a diamond, Its more grey than black I thought. The smell of coal dust filled my nostrils and chest and made me want to cough and sneeze, I put my hand over my mouth to prevent this.

I thought about my father who worked underground everyday and wrinkled my nose in disgust, I don't want to work in the mines when I'm older I mutter to myself, I'm getting bored now, feels like I been here hours, I'm freezing, my hands are cold, I examine my gloves which have two big holes in the fingers. I need new gloves but don't want to ask mum as money is tight. It's gone quiet now, can't hear any shouting, I look up towards the entrance of the hole and that's when I saw it, a shoe, a great big black shiny shoe. I hold my breath, too scared to breathe, a face appears now and looks down at me, a kind young face with spiky ginger hair, 'It can't be a policeman,' I think to myself, I had heard my dad talk about the police, how they were nasty and hit the miners with truncheons and locked them up, he didn't look like a pig either. But it is the police, I can see his uniform now. I stared back at him waiting for him to speak, he didn't, he just smiled. I noticed that he had a tooth missing, 'wonder if that happened in the picketing,' I think to myself, he winks at me now, "no one down here Alf," he shouts before giving me another grin and disappearing.

The sound of engines starting fill my ears, I was still too scared to move though, my bum was freezing and my feet were wet and cold. I could smell chip fat and knew it must be 1pm, that's when Enid the fish shop opened, my belly rumbled in response to the smell. I was scared too, scared my brother had gone home and left me, I could imagine my sister and horrible Julie sitting there laughing because I was lost, I started to cry now.

"There you are squirt" came my brothers voice as he

appeared over the hole, "I've been looking for you cm-on lets go". I wiped my eyes and quickly jumped out of the hole, I blinked as the light hurt my eyes but welcomed the fresh air, "grab a bag and run before they come back," commanded my brother. I grabbed a sack but it was too heavy for me to lift, I dragged the sack, running as quickly as I could behind my brother and Dai who had reappeared, stopping every now and then to pull my trousers up.

We were home in minutes, my sister was still sat where we had left her, I dragged the sack through the living room. It felt lighter now, then I noticed it, a big gaping hole in the bottom of the sack, half of my coal was gone. My sister and awful Julie started giggling at the look of horror on my face, "well done squirt," my brother piped up "we filled 21 sacks of coal today which will see us through the winter, you also hid from the pigs, wait till I tell dad he'll be so proud," he shot my sister a warning look and the giggling stopped. I feel myself fill with pride, so much, I feel I will burst, I wasn't going to tell him that the policeman had seen me, or that my sack had a hole, that would be my secret. I turned to my sister and poked out my tongue.

Natalie, 1984, snapshot taken from the video 'All Out.'

Phillip Rosser – The Wheel of Misfortune

Phillip is from Penrhiwceiber and was sixteen when he started his career as an apprentice engineer in the Nantgarw Colliery in South Wales, he passed out as an electrician in 1981.

We knew the strike was going to happen; we came out about two weeks before everyone else, then the whole of the South Wales just came out on strike. In the beginning it was just euphoria, it was just 'here we go,' we would go with the flow.

Picketing away didn't come until about two or three months into the strike it was then that we saw the other half of it, something we would never see in the valleys. In the valleys nearly everyone was out on strike but the places where we were sent it was totally the opposite. There was Father against Son, Brother against Brother and town versus town, half was on strike the other half wasn't, it was a different ball game now.

In June or July we were sent to picket Littleton Colliery in Stafford it was chaos, we were not allowed to talk to the scabs to try and reason with them, we had no freedom of speech, this right had been taken away from us. The police were horrible and ready for trouble. The miners arranged a meeting in a local pub, we needed a plan, a plan was drawn up to climb the head gear to stop the pit from functioning, me and my butty drew the short straw and we agreed to climb the head gear. Little did I know then but what happened next would change my life forever and certainly not for the better.

A short while later we jumped the gates in the colliery and ran towards the shaft, the scabs were close on our heels pulling us back, we were fighting like fuck, desperate to climb the head gear. We finally did and managed to get to the top where it was vertical, we shouted, "right, now you need to shut the pit", the pit had to be shut as us being there was endangering lives as there were men on the winding gear. We planned to remain there for a couple of hours to stop the pit but little did we know we would be there for much longer.

Des Duckfield the South Wales Executive came to see us the next day, he climbed all the way up to where we were, he was scared of heights and by the time he reached us could barely talk as he was shaking so much. He asked us if we would consider staying up there for a couple of days and we agreed. In total we remained at the top of the head gear for four whole days. The publicity was enormous we appeared on news at ten and the ground was littered with press. We were given no food or water for the whole of the time we were up there despite protests from Duckfield and other officials for them to do so, even prisoners on death row are entitled to food and water but not us miners we had nothing.

When we finally decided to come down we were promised by the police that we would not be harmed, the promise meant nothing to them because as soon as our feet touched the ground the violence started, a policeman jumped on top of me and thumped me numerous times before dragging me into the police van. We were taken to the cells and stripped naked of all our clothing, we were then hosed with cold water. The force of the water sent me stumbling and I fell over and split my head open. We were thrown into separate cells; I received no medical treatment for my injury.

I was kept locked up for three days in total whilst in police custody and I was constantly taunted, the police would come into the cell every hour day and night often disturbing me from my sleep, they would place a pillow over my face and thump me as hard as they could, all of the time calling me a Welsh fucker. I was in despair in the end I just didn't know what to do, there was no point fighting back as the consequences would be worse. I received this treatment for the remainder of the time I was there, resulting in a black eye and bruising to my face.

When I appeared in court I was reunited with my butty, it was obvious he had received the same brutal treatment as me as he too was covered in bruises, he said, "Oh Phil this is fucking hard innit," to which I replied,

"keep your head up butt," I just didn't know what else to say, how had it come to this? I can honestly say it was the hardest time of my life.

I remember our Barrister coming over, a long haired quite scruffy man from London, the NUM had sent him, he obviously knew what had gone on as he said to me, "don't worry they wont hurt you no more" and they didn't, well at least not in Littleton anyway. After this we were sacked, we were charged and found guilty of endangering lives, we received a two year prison sentence suspended for two years, we were also given a £2,500 fine.

You think I would have stopped there, but no, not me, a week after court I was back, I was no longer a miner, well, not officially anyway but I still wanted to fight for what I believed so strongly in even though I no longer had a job to fight for, my fellow workers and the generation after them did so I continued.

This time the journey took us to Orgreave power station and all I can describe it as is a fucking massacre. The bus picked me up and was full of big muscly miners who you wouldn't want to pick a fight with. The mood was jovial on our way up even though we were stopped eighteen times in total by the police, eight times before we got to Hirwaun, obviously the police knew our plans. We knew deep down as we made our way up that we had to succeed, if we didn't we would lose this strike, we had to stop the power station, we just had to.

That night was a warm night, we met up with other miners, hundreds of them from different towns, all different but all fighting the same cause, chatting by bonfires under the stars. I remember one person in particular, a man called Arthur from Nottingham, in his village there were only six of them on strike and believe you me they were treated very bad, beaten up, spat at and taunted on the streets, very different to the valleys. In the morning we were awoken around 6 am by none other than Arthur Scargill, "c'mon lads" he said, he stood on a soap box and fair play he gave a fantastic speech that motivated us miners, he had noticed my black eye and said, "Look at that boy from Nantgarw still with a black eye from being beaten by the police" little did he know that the black eye I was sporting hadn't been at the hands of the police this time but a very hard cricket ball. Scargill then encouraged us to raise our banners and together we started our march to the power station. There was a mist on our way down the mountain and as the mist began to rise we were faced with a sea of black, rows and rows of black, the police were waiting for us. There were around 18,000 miners in total and around 50,000 police they were determined we were not going to get to the power station.

The police were all kitted out in full riot gear and us miners, well, we were just in shorts and daps, after all it was bloody boiling. I seen a lot that day as I had to keep out of the way, after all I did have a suspended sentence hanging over me, so I climbed a tree and took in the horrors that unfolded around me.

Around 1pm the snatch squad arrived, the snatch squad is where the police would go into the crowd and snatch unsuspecting miners and arrest them for no reason at all. That day a man also saw his brother, he was a serving soldier in the forces on the picket line with the police. The news didn't surprise me as there were rows of police officers lined up with no numbers displayed on their uniforms, and then all of a sudden, I'm not kidding, now all hell broke loose. The police hit their riot shields together it must have been some sort of plan as they just attacked, they hit everybody in their sight with their truncheons. Hundreds of dogs on leads appeared and started biting the miners their teeth piercing and ripping at their clothing and skin. Then to top it all off police on horses emerged, they were the biggest horses I have ever seen in my life. They charged at the miners knocking them to the floor before trampling over them, if this was not enough the police man on horse back would then bludgeon the defenceless miner lying on the floor. A police man came face to face with me, I got nervous, I didn't want any trouble and I started laughing, don't ask me why but I always laugh when I'm nervous. He started getting angry and I knew I was about to be arrested "run," shouted the Yorkshire lad who was with me, so we ran through an alley the police right behind. An elderly lady was on her back door and beckoned to us to run in for safety, no sooner had we shut the front door the police were there kicking it open, they pushed the elderly lady out of the way swinging their truncheons as they moved towards us.

A police man hit the Yorkshire lad several times across the head with his truncheon before turning his attention to me, he jumped on top of me, pinning me to the floor with his knees on my shoulders, "fucking laughing at me was you!" he didn't give me chance to reply just started repeatedly sticking the head into me. I got up covered in blood, the Yorkshire lad was in a bad way bleeding from the ears. The old lady was terrified, she had no phone to call for medical help, but, luckily for us a doctor lived next door to her, she kindly got him to attend to us.

The doctor turned up accompanied by his daughter who immediately screamed in terror when she saw our injuries. The doctor took us to hospital, as we passed in the car I witnessed miners being beaten in the street in front of horrified shoppers, it was horrific, something I had never seen before and most certainly do not want to see again. I received 10 stitches to my head and bruising to my face and body. I heard afterwards that the Yorkshire lad received a fractured skull. If the policeman or soldier who carried out this attack on me apologized to me today and asked for forgiveness, my reply would be, to fuck right off.

The bus picked me up at the hospital for my journey back to South Wales, moral was low, sadness tinged the air, every single one of these big burly men carried a wound from the Orgreave massacre, big hard men with cuts, black eyes and bruises. I knew then the strike was over, we had lost (although the strike continued for another six months afterwards). I think I am the only man left now from that bus full of miners all the rest have passed away, I am the only one left who can tell you the truth of the horrors the Nantgarw miners witnessed at Orgreave that day. How lives were not lost in this battle I will never know, but what I do know is that on that day the miners were battered, bitten, trampled and totally humiliated by the police and the Tory Government.

However I did get my own back on the police a short while after, we were picketing at our own pit in Nantgarw, it was relatively quiet down there, about 40 picketers and 200 police, there was only one scab who we would holler at as he turned up for his shift. Some of the old miners had a fair relationship with the police, they would chat and drink tea with them, not me though, I wouldn't associate with them.

They dropped the police presence in Nantgarw down to fifty as it was quiet, but, lo and behold on the very day of the drop two buses full of Abercynon boys turned up at the pit, on board were big Lukey and Sluggy two big local lads. I'm not kidding now, but there was fucking ructions down there, at the time there was a Japanese film crew present they were rushing around panic stricken. The police were outnumbered, they'd had it easy here, but on this day they had to earn their coin. The taxi carrying the scab was turned upside down and fights between police officers and miners broke out, even the old miners, who days before had shared tea with the officers were now getting stuck in. Don't get me wrong, I am not condoning violence but what happened that day was nothing compared to the violence the police inflicted on the miners. Needless to say the police were back to 200 the very next day.

I think to myself sometimes, 'was it all worth it?' The violence that was inflicted on me and the violence I witnessed fellow miners receive, will stay with me for the rest of my days. The strike ruined me, my career as an electrician was no more, I became blacklisted, every job I was interviewed for turned me down flat due to my criminal record, I lost my pension, could not receive benefits for a while and had no help from anyone. All this for what? For trying to secure our own jobs and jobs for the future generation. We were treated like lepers by the police, worse than the fucking IRA, punched by them for no reason at all and all the time they were getting richer, they would have liked the strike to last for longer as the police were filling their wallets on the miners suffering. Saying this, if I had to, I would probably do it all over again.

Carol White

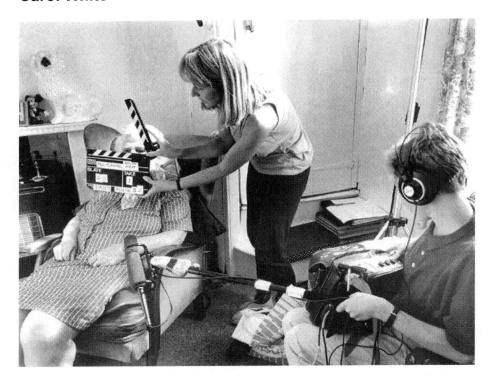

Carol was a filmmaker involved with Channel 4 community workshops; Chapter Arts in Cardiff was a part of it. Being involved with the women's film workshop gave her the idea of getting involved with the miner's wives. She was going to demonstrations anyway and got friendly with the Maerdy miner's wives, creating a documentary film entitled "Someone else in the house." Carol now works for Grass Roots in Cardiff. The film is available from the archives at South Wales Mining Museum in Swansea.

Most of my time during demonstrations was spent running

around with a huge camera and tripod trying to get shots of the

crowd; I had to get ahead of them to be able to shoot. The

name of the film came from something said by one of the

miner's wives interviewed, she jokes that their husbands now

think there's "Someone else in the house." This was because

the women had become so heavily involved in the strike action,

and were now politically motivated, their previous role as 'just a

housewife' had changed dramatically. At a Christmas party

with the Maerdy women everyone got up and thanked us for

our support, I was overwhelmed and cried as I told them, "No, thank you, for standing up for your rights."

Another group I became involved with was in Onllwyn in the Neath Valley, the following story is about the involvement of the gay and lesbian community in London and how both sides had to overcome their own unfounded prejudices at the time. Names have been changed to protect privacy and the terms used are in no way derogatory, they were used after a national newspaper thought they were being clever, but the group turned it around and kept the name. The 'Dirty Thirty' up in Leicester did exactly the same.

Pits and Perverts

"You have worn our badge 'coal not dole' and you know what harassment means, as we do. Now we will pin your badge on us, we will support you. It won't change overnight, but, now 140,000 miners know that there are other causes and other problems. We know about blacks and gays and nuclear disarmament and we will never be the same." David Donovan, NUM 1984.

One of the oddest sights in the Swansea Valley during the 1984/85 miners strike was the Onllwyn Miners' Support Group's minibus. Emblazoned boldly on the side of the van, often full of beefy strikers on their way to the picket line, were these words;

Provided by, "The Lesbian and Gay Men Support The Miners – London"

The van symbolised and was the inspiration for this endearing story of what happened when the traditional mining community of Onllwyn was forced to confront its own preconceptions and prejudices when a group of gay London men raised money for the isolated Welsh village's strike fund.

This clash between the two seemingly alien cultures would develop into a sometimes painful, often funny, but always illuminating journey through changing attitudes to final acceptance and understanding.

Initial prejudices were not exclusively on the miners' side. The gay men also had their own preconceptions. Whilst they revered the miners as 'working class heroes,' they also feared them as ultra macho, beer swilling, rugby playing 'he men.'

It was at the Miners Welfare Hall that the Strike Committee first announced that the London Gay Community had made a collection. Cat calls and whistles soon turned into a stunned silence however, when the meeting heard of the massive amount that had been collected. Jokes continued but eventually a decision was taken to invite the gay men to the village to present their cheque.

Thus began what was to become an enduring friendship between these two unlikely communities. The first visit was traumatic for both parties but during the year of the strike the two groups would make many visits to one another. Whilst the miners' prejudices dissolved slowly, it was with the women of the village, who during the strike had started to challenge their own traditional role, that the strongest links were forged.

Soon the women were travelling throughout the country to speak and fundraise on behalf of their communities. When in London they would stay with the members of this very 'urbane' gay community and were introduced to London's nightlife. Some of the stories that followed are legendary. The social climax of these visits was the famous 'Pits and Perverts' benefit which was held at the Electric Ballroom, Camden and featured Jimmy Somerville and The Bronski Beat.

On the return visits the gay men found themselves 'tin kettling' with the women, witnessing the rustling of sheep from the mountain top and attending the village school's eisteddfod. The relationship between the two groups of men was more difficult. For a lot of the miners in the earlier days it meant having to watch what they said, as well as protecting the gay men from the homophobic attitude of others. They were also confused about the warmth of feeling between their wives and these men. Valleys men are not renowned for their understanding of platonic relationships.

Their feelings came to a head at a committee meeting where they debated into the night about what should be written on the side of their newly acquired mini-bus. When the tribute was suggested, many of the men felt that they would be poked fun at as they drove around in it. It was one of the women who pointed out in no uncertain terms, the hypocrisy of their attitude and eventually the meeting unanimously agreed to the slogan being painted. Slowly, through personal contact, prejudice was further eroded until a large contingent of Onllwyn miners decided to attend the Gay Pride march of 1985.

Woven through this theme of the joining of the two communities is the personal story of Susan, her husband Melvyn and David who was billeted to them on that first Onllwyn visit. Despite the terrible hardships of that year, the strike had been a gift to Susan. Confined to the traditional role of wife and mother, she had grown both politically and in confidence as the strike went on. Like many other women, the year had seen her flower.

David, a teacher, was well read and had travelled. He showed Susan a wider horizon. A strong relationship grew between the two and David set about trying to guide Susan into realising her potential. Melvyn, like a lot of the men, was firstly suspicious and then jealous of the growing bond between David and his wife. He was however, supportive of Susan's new ambitions.

The friendship between the communities continued throughout the year of the strike and onwards. Every year the gay men would return to the Welfare Hall for a reunion, but one year David was missing. Susan discovered that he was in hospital suffering from Aids. She rushed to see him and to take him the long promised photograph of her graduation from Swansea University. Susan visited him weekly until the end.

At David's funeral, friends told stories and poems were read. Onllwyn paid him one final visit. Melvyn helped carry his coffin and the miners of course, sang.

There in Spirit - John Pritchard

John started working in the mines when he was 33 years old, he worked in Bargoed, Brittania and Bedwas. He was unable to go back to mining after an accident in Bedwas Colliery. After a long recovery process, John went to work for Shelter Cymru until he retired. He is now an active member of his community in Bargoed, receiving the 'Green Flag' award for 'The Tarragon project,' and an award from the Queen in 2013. The project involved turning a brownfield site into a substantial community allotment site, enabling local community groups and members to grow their own fresh food.

Bargoed pit was extremely hard work, we were working in a seam that was only 3ft high and 18 inches of that was water. We were paid, 1/6d water money per day, equivalent to seven and a half new pence in today's money. Conditions were awful, we wanted more money, but top wack was 37 1/2p and money for wellies. I remember once we found a fossil tree in The South Pit, the manager came in and told us to blow it up, if we had to get the museum involved we would have had to stop work. We had to walk for two hours to get to the face and two hours back, that part was hardly viable, so I can understand why they closed it. 600 men were at Bargoed, luckily other pits absorbed most of the jobs that were lost through that closure.

I started work in Brittania pit after Bargoed closed, during the 1970's I picketed during the strike that we won. In this strike we had a proper ballot, the majority wanted to go out. I was indirectly affected by the 1984 strike, but what upset me most was that 84 men had come out without being given a vote. The strike in fact was illegal, which is why we didn't get the support from other industries, if it had been balloted properly it would have become a general strike.

Scargill didn't want the pits to close, but I think he was a bit of a Marxist and wanted to overthrow the government. I still think that Scargill was the wrong man for the job politically, there was too much tension between him and Thatcher after she overthrew the Heath government.

I spent two years in hospital and rehabilitation recovering from a broken back, caused from an accident underground. I had to learn to walk all over again. But I wasn't the only one, there were hundreds of miners in similar situations, I made many friends at The Talygarn Miners Rehabilitation Centre. If we hadn't been in there we would have been picketing with the rest of our colleagues. We were fighting against pit closures, the intention to close pits that were still commercially viable was wrong. I agree some pits had to close, but there were others that could have been made profitable. Although Scargill was a good orator, he made things worse by prophesising mass closures, he lost sight of the real issues and made it personal.

Being on the picket lines wasn't easy, there was continuous police harassment to deal with. "Who's shagging your wife, whilst you're here then?" was just one of many taunts. The use of the army was suspected at the time by many, it 's presence was witnessed first hand by others who actually recognised friends or family. *In 2013 after a 30 year embargo on official documents was lifted, confirmation of the army's presence was finally proved.*

The miners fought hard for work that was hard and dirty, the pay they received was well deserved. Many families for the first time found that they had enough money to buy their own cars and houses and also afford to send their children to university. The result of the 1984/85 strike was disappointing and tragic for the families who could no longer keep up payments on a mortgage or pay for higher education for their children. Divorce rocketed and many families were split forever. Those who were lucky enough to find new jobs were usually poorly paid in comparison.

National Archives: Margaret Thatcher was days from calling out troops during miners' strike, documents show

Ministers considered ordering an emergency recall of Parliament to pass a new law giving extra powers for soldiers to replace striking workers, papers from 1984 made public by the National Archives disclose.

This excerpt is from The Telegraph in January 2014: Sam Marsden reports.

Ray Davies – The Price of Coal

Councillor Ray Davies, now in his 80's, is still a very prominent activist for many causes including helping to found The Rhymney Valley Miners' Support Group during the 1984/85 strike.

Over many decades he has fought against injustice, he was vice chair of CND Wales, and an active trade unionist, receiving an award for his work. Ray went to Palestine seven times and was shot in the head. He campaigned against the Iraq war, smuggling in medical help, but was arrested on his return. Ray was also jailed several times for his objection and refusal to pay the Poll Tax. In January 2009 at a Gaza demo in London he was assaulted by riot police at the age of 79, he received compensation in 2011.

Known as 'Red Ray' by many, for his politics and his famous red beret, he is a larger than life character and an inspiration to us all.

Ray has also written a book with the help of his wife Wendy, commemorating the Miners' Strike of 1984/85, (*A Miner's Life,* published by Tower Press.)

He has kindly allowed us to include his personal story as a boy miner in this book. Let us never forget, 'The Price of Coal.'

Health and safety issues have always been a prevalent theme on the issues of working underground. After the disaster in Senghenydd at Universal Colliery in 1901, when 81 miners lost their lives, you would have thought that lessons would have been learnt and precautionary measures would have been taken to prevent another such incident. But, no, just 12 years later the worst disaster in the history of Britain occurred, at the same pit, Universal. That day 439 men and boys, fathers, children, sons and brothers were lost to the mining community of Senghenydd. Between the years of 1913 and 2011, the Gleision mine disaster the most recent, a further 183 miners lost their lives. (Welsh Coalmines.co.uk/Disasters) So unfortunately no lessons were learned, profit came before the safety of human lives as usual.

A Boy Miner's Life – The Price of Coal

It was November, 1943. Standing in front of the whole school at half term in Coed-y-Brain Boys' School, Llanbradach, were the 38 who were about to leave school. As was the custom, our Head teacher went around each of the boys and found something nice to say about most of them.

When he came to me, his whole demeanour changed:

"Here is Ray Davies, who threw an inkwell at the teacher, ruining his clothes; and who then jumped out of the classroom through the front window. Here is the boy who refused to do his school work and was sent to the remedial class. This is the ruffian who broke into the school and painted rude swear words about the teacher . Despite receiving corrective caning throughout his school life, he has never changed. Perhaps his life working underground as a miner will change him, but I doubt it." No handshake for Ray.

Back home, gran was waiting with two sacks. "We need more coal, and now is the best time to get it". Up on the colliery coal sidings, 30 trunks of prime Welsh coal was waiting to be transported to Cardiff docks. "Up you jump, Ray, and throw down as much as you can-as quick as you can!" Within 10 minutes we filled half a hundredweight sack for me and one Cwt for gran. Making our way down the Pit road, young Hayden Morgan shouted, "The pit sergeant is around the corner!" We quickly threw the coal bags into the brambles and pretended to collect stick kindling for firewood.

"What trouble are you getting up to now, Davies?" said Sergeant Watts, holding my ear.

"Nothing, sir, nothing, honest, sir." I replied. "Make sure you don't then", he said. When the coast was finally clear, we sneaked through the back lanes of Thomas Street , and home to 16 Lewis Terrace and a warm fire.

On the following Monday at 7 a.m., I walked up to Llanbradach colliery, where I was met by Mr. Keen, in charge of the coal screening operations. Coal tubs coming up from the pit first went to the check weigher. The numbers on the side of the tram decided which miner received the payment. Then on to the tumblers where the coal trams were turned upside down onto a judding slide and on to a steel conveyer belt. "Start taking stones and rubbish off the belt, and be quick about it". I was too short to reach the conveyer and had to stand on a wooden box. After about ten minutes a bell sounded, and coal stopped coming off the chute. "Get up to the tumbler quick and unblock the belt," screamed Mr. Keen. I crept with two other young lads through the dark hold with steel bars, on the juddering chute. Two large boulders of coal were jammed together. We prised our bars between them, and all of a sudden there was a roar and a rush of coal. We were bowled off our feet and onto the belt, battered, bleeding and bruised. After first aid, I went straight up to Mr. Ellis Hughes, manager of the pit, and begged to work in the mine. "No", he said, " you're too small and puny. Get back to school."

Every day for a week I ambushed Mr. Hughes, and begged him to let me go underground, until at last he gave in. He wrote out a short note to the lamp room, where I was given my first oil lamp No. 153. My first weeks' pay from the screens was one pound, 5 shillings. I proudly gave this to my Dad who gave me 2s/6d pocket money and sent to the local outfitters to be measured up for my first suit. On the following Monday at 5:30 am I walked up the Graddfa road to the colliery lamp room, and with my oil lamp, amongst hundreds of men and boy miners, I presented myself to the Fireman for cigarette and match searching . I ignored his hurtful remark, "What are you doing out of school?" and jumped into the cage. With the gates closed, we hurtled down the shaft at a terrific speed. By the time we hit bit bottom my legs were like rubber. We walked past the pit horse stables, and on to the fireman. I was upset when we passed a huge dram with a horse that had been killed on the night shift.

The fireman checked my lamp and told me my miner was Harry Morgan from Senghenydd. It took us 3/4 hour to reach our first resting point, walking up and down hills. The dust was overpowering, getting into my eyes, nose and throat. We sat down for ten minutes, and slaked our thirst and washed down the dust. Most of the miners were either ardent communists or left wing socialists. I listened to the political arguments, about the need to take control of the economy, the banks, railway, mines, our own lives and future. I was

131

enthralled. The fire that was burning in my belly was burning fiercely. I joined the Young Communist League and was determined to play my part in changing the world.

I came down to earth with a thud when we reached the coalface. Harry Morgan gave me a pick and a shovel and told me to cut coal and fill the tubs (drams). The shovel was so heavy, every time I smashed the pick into the coal I thought my arms would come out of my shoulder. I did my best for Harry, but working in a narrow 3'6" space nearly killed me. After three hours, we stopped for ten minutes .I stuffed two sandwiches of bread and beef dripping and three of jam into me, then back on the coalface. Harry shouted at me that I was throwing more coal on the floor than in the dram. At 1:30 , with my back in two, we put our tools in the tool bar and trudged out to pit bottom. Into the cage, and back to the surface. The sun blinded me. I cadged a cigarette off my mate and thought of that beautiful school which I hated, but which I now would have given my eye teeth to go back to.

I arrived home; my gran had taken the tin tub from the back yard and poured in the hot water. Then my dad washed his top half, followed by my brother, leaving me the lukewarm water to wash in. My gran topped up the bath with more hot water, and dad and George washed their bottom half, leaving me to wash in sludge. During this daily ritual, aunties, girl cousins, every Tom Dick and Harry kept walking past us as we were naked. No one took any notice, since every home went through the same ritual. My gran took one look at me and took me to the cold water tap outside, and scrubbed me all over. She sent me straight to bed, exhausted, but not before I had a clip across the ear from dad for turning down the one safe job on the surface.

After one week, Harry Morgan refused to keep me as his boy miner. He told the Fireman that we couldn't fill enough coal to pay his wages and mine, and that I was a liability. I went home and cried with shame. The following Monday I presented my lamp to the Fireman. "What am I to do with you?" he said. When everyone went off to their respective coal face sections, I meekly followed Mr. Knight on his round. We called on a Cardiff publican who was working in the pit instead of the Army. Sam Knight, the foreman, whispered in Stan Jenkins' ear.

Afterwards Mr. Knight said, "Mr. Jenkins will take you under his wing whilst he is working on minimum wage preparing this new coalface for piece work. It will take at least four weeks, and if by then your work rate has improved, he will keep you on as his boy miner".

So Stan Jenkins took me on as his boy miner. Working at the coalface, he taught me my trade: how to cut a wooden pit prop to pin up the creaking roof; how to bore shot firing holes true and straight ; testing the roof and checking for gas. Some of the other boy miners made fun of me. They jumped on me, and pulled down my trousers. I fought back at every one of them; and even though they were stronger and older, and always managed to get the better of me, I won their respect. I worked my fingers to the bone: laying tram lines, moving piles of rock, and cutting out slag infested coal seams. I went home every evening and practiced my shovelling. I was determined to prove my worth as a boy miner.

On our first week on piece work, we filled 5 drams of best Welsh coal a day, which more than paid both our wages. One of Stan's tips was to cut a 2" groove beneath the coal seam, so the weight of the coal above would weaken the seam But once, just after I cut the groove, there was a loud cracking sound. "Look out!" screamed Stan, but it was too late. A massive amount of coal came crashing down on me. "Well done, young Ray. You've cut enough coal to fill five drams- but I think you've broken your leg." So it was off to hospital for me (again). A broken foot and leg meant ten weeks off work, with a pittance of pay.

Whilst working with Stan, the government started to send every 10th conscripted new recruit to the forces down to the pits. It was the brainchild of Labour MP Ernie Bevan, who wanted coat output to double. Each new Bevan boy was given two months training, given new boots, gloves, overalls, and helmets. I was angry that these 18 year old Bevan boys were having perks. I went up to Mr. Hughes , the manager, and asked for 3 months' training and all the other perks: especially new pit boots and overalls. I was wearing my granddad's trousers (he was 6 feet tall) with the legs cut down, leaving the crotch of the trousers sagging down to my knees. The manager gave me a filthy look and threatened to kick my ass if I didn't get back to work.

" All right", I muttered, "but just supposing I had another grievance. How would I go about calling a strike?"

"Well, you stay outside the lamproom. Stop all the men going down to the divi. Explain the grievance, call for a vote, and refuse to work until you win your case." Wow, I thought. The next morning I stood outside the lamp room. I told all the other boy miners not to go down the pit. A strike for better conditions must be won. Justice for boy miners. Down with the bosses! was my clarion call, and we went off up the mountain. We climbed trees, went bird nesting, stole apples out of the pit manager's garden,, smoked fags and played follow my leader. The strike lasted a week.. When my dad held out his hand for my wages, there were none. A good hiding followed, not because of the strike, but because I lied to him and did not confide in him.

"You will be victimised, just like I was".

"I don't care, dad. You didn't when it happened to you. Justice is justice. United we stand, divided we fall. Isn't that what you have always taught me?" I saw a tear in his eye.

I went back to work on Monday, and so ended the first of many fights against the bosses. When I returned to the pit, Stan Jenkins had been transferred to another pit and I was allocated to work with a fantastic, hardworking miner , Fred Smith. He was happy go lucky, with a nice young family. We were soon amongst the top coal cutting and filling teams down the pit.

Life for us boy miners followed a regular pattern. Up a 5 a.m. at the sound of the pit siren: 4 blasts at 5 a.m., 6 at 5:30, and one long blast at 5:45. We rushed up Graddfa road, to fill our jacks (tin water cans) from the sweet stream opposite the footbridge by the railway line. The tramp of miners' hobnailed boots, going to work on the morning shift, mingled with those of the weary night shift workers trudging home. We then bought our daily screw of chewing tobacco from the wooden hut just outside the pit offices. Most of us chewed the addictive tobacco to keep the coal dust from our lungs. We picked up our lamps; my number, 153, is engraved in my memory. If these were not back on the shelf opposite your number by 3 p.m., all hell let loose, and search parties would be formed.

Into the cage we went. At pit bottom, a Fireman checked the lamp, and on to the coal face for a day of back breaking hard work in appalling conditions. At 2 p.m., the shift over, our tools went back on the bar. There was a rush to the pit bottom, dodging journeys of coal drams to go back into the cage. On reaching the surface, the day was over for the miner, but not for the boys. We had to take our pick axe heads to the blacksmith's shop for sharpening, in readiness for the next day's toil, and then call in to Mr Parish, the ironmonger on Lewis Terrace, for lumps of chalk to mark the drams with the miner's identifying number.

I was back home usually by 3:30, but I was often late for the bath tub ritual with brother George and dad, so my bath was even colder. For recreation we had films at the cinema youth club, Ted Tim's boxing club, monthly Young communist meetings, and Army cadet training. On Saturdays and Sundays we played rugby and football.

Some awful accidents occurred below surface. I was helping John Davies, a young haulier to hitch up a new pit pony to the dram of coal which Fred and I had filled, when things went horribly wrong. The haulier had just managed to harness the horse to the dram, but before he could jump out of the way, the horse reared up, knocking the young man to the floor. The horse then dragged the full dram over John. The screams could be heard miles away. I ran in front of the horse, and beat it with a steel bar to stop it dragging the dram further over John's battered body. Fred leapt on to the dram and eventually pulled out the dram connecting pin, and the horse leapt forward, lashed out at me with his rear hooves, breaking my leg. Other miners came on the scene and helped unload the dram, and eventually retrieved the badly injured haulier. I was left on the floor, quietly crying, not because of my injury, but because I thought that John was dead. We both ended up in Caerphilly Miners Hospital, where I was plastered up and sent home. John spent 15 months in hospital with multiple injuries. He eventually recovered but never worked again.

Grievances were brewing amongst the men. The coal seam was difficult, and nothing was being done to reduce the risk from the deadly dust. Too many accidents, and too many men killed. Fred and I went to a meeting at the Workmen's Institute. That night our Union rep and an executive member- a firebrand like Arthur Scargill- addressed the meeting and told us, " The solution is in your own hands. You can sit back and let the bosses walk all over you, or you can stand together and fight." There were huge cheers.

"All in favour of one last try to get the bosses to see sense - and if we fail, industrial action". Dad, Fred and I shot our hands up in favour. Just one or two older miners voted no. When no concessions came out of the meetings, we found ourselves on strike. One of our leaders was arrested on the picket line and put in the cells in Llanbradach. Out on the picket line, there was a great feeling of determination and solidarity. Fred said, "We will win!".

There were three pits: the House Coal, where I and my brother George worked; the Four Foot, where dad worked, and the Nine Foot where brother Leslie worked. I asked Fred why we were standing outside the entry to the pit. "We are here to stop any scabs from going to work".

"What the hell is a scab?"

"A scab is nothing more than a piece of excrement , a rat, a traitor, a back stabbing bastard. He would watch you starve and take the bread out of your kids' mouths. He would sell his soul to the devil for three pence." I had never heard Fred swear before.

"OK, OK,", I said. "I get the point." The word Scab provoked such an outburst from that kind, caring, tolerant man that the impression stayed with me for the rest of my life. Just to emphasise his point, Fred gave me a copy of Jack London's famous definition of a scab. Scabs have been called many things by many people during the course of labour history, but Jack London's description of the scab: written with barbed wire on sandpaper, easily dwarfs all others.

"After God had finished the rattlesnake, the toad, the vampire, He had some awful substance left with which he made a scab.

A scab is a two-legged animal with a cork-screw soul, a water-logged brain, a combination backbone of jelly and glue. Where others have hearts, he carries a tumor of rotten principles.

When a scab comes down the street, men turn their backs and angels weep in heaven, and the Devil shuts the gates of Hell to keep him out.

No man has a right to scab so long as there is a pool of water to drown his carcass in, or a rope long enough to hang his body with. Judas Iscariot was a gentleman compared with a scab. For betraying his master, he had character enough to hang himself. A scab has not.

Esau sold his birthright for a mess of pottage. Judas Iscariot sold his Savior for thirty pieces of silver. Benedict Arnold sold his country for a promise of a commission in the British Army. The modern strikebreaker sells his birthright, his country, his wife, his children and his fellow men for an unfulfilled promise from his employer, trust or corporation.

Esau was a traitor to himself: Judas Iscariot was a traitor to his God; Benedict Arnold was a traitor to his country; a strikebreaker is a traitor to his God, his country, his wife, his family and his class."

Later on in the day, a large contingent of police turned up.

"Who are these men?" said Sam Norris, who led the picket line.

"They are our heavies, to keep you bunch of trouble makers in order," answered our local police constable.

It soon became clear why they were there. Three lorries turned up, one carrying steel colliery arches, and 2 with large timber props. When the drivers refused to turn back, the miners moved into the road to stop them. I went to join them, but Dad grabbed hold of me. "No, not yet, son. Blood will be spilt today and I don't want it to be yours." The only woman on the scene picked up a large stone and threw it at the police. I immediately did the same. Fortunately for me, the police were more interested in arresting the woman than bothering with small fry like me. Dad however gave me a clip across the ear. "You don't win strikes by being stupid. We will win by the strength of our case, our determination and solidarity."

"But dad," I complained, rubbing my tingling ear. "Mrs. Jones threw a stone".

"Yes, but her husband is wrongfully in prison".
With that, we all joined in to protect Mrs. Jones and smuggle her out of the crowd, away from the thug police.

Eventually, the bosses wanted to settle the strike, but no one would negotiate because our chief negotiator was in jail. The bosses went into the cell and tried to persuade our union leader to settle, arguing that we were damaging the war effort.

We point blank refused their meagre offer and told them that they were not going to win the war by blackmailing the miners or by paying us starvation wages. Our leader was quickly released from prison, and all our moderate demands were settled. Everyone was overjoyed, except us boys. Our 10 days off work had brought the colour back to our cheeks: we played Tarzan in the mountain, swam in the quarry pond, played football. We even got a resolution passed, and our small Communist meeting supported the strike.

Back at the coalface, there were lots of small rock falls to clear and pit props to replace before we could think of digging coal. Whilst we were having our ten minute snap (food break), there was a huge commotion some 200 yards up the coalface.

Fred and I rushed with our picks and shovels, to find a large roof fall on the new coal road heading. Miners who were first on the scene were already digging like mad and had taken enough of the small rocks off to see the repairer who lay beneath the fall; but before we could pull him free, a second roof fall came down which killed him outright. When at last we recovered the body, I saw it was Ben, a 6'6" Bevan boy from West London. His butty and senior repairer told us that the poor lad did not have the experience to respond to the cracking sounds from the roof and left it too late to jump.

Ben was one of the 18 year old Bevan boys who had good training, helmets and gloves. He was far too tall to work in the 3'6" coalface, and so worked on repairing. I hated him at first, jealous of what I thought was preferential treatment over us boys. I soon had got to know him. He told me that all his family supported the Tories, but working with us in the mine changed all his previously held convictions. He was now a full blown socialist and attended all lodge meetings. He told me that his mother was overjoyed that he was selected for the pit and so missed the call up. He was much safer here than in the trenches.

The management allowed two of the miners time off to go and break the news gently to his family. What comradeship, what a wonderful community we had then. We had very little, but what we had, we shared, and we looked out for one another. And our kind, considerate bosses docked the two miners' pay for taking the sad news to Ben's home.

Working on the coalface was so very hard. By the time snap time had come, I was already exhausted. On one shift, after playing rugby the previous day and following a sleepless night, I was at the coalface. We had filled 3 drams, cut 5 props for the roof, and bored a shot firing hole by hand, ready for the 2 to 10 shift. Fred and I sat down to eat our snap. A small amount of gas was in the air; consequently I fell asleep with a half eaten jam sandwich in my mouth. Kind hearted Fred left me there for an extra ten minutes. He knew I had a boxing match with the Army Cadet boys that night.

Whilst he was working at the top end of the coalface, Sam Knight came by. Seeing me sleeping, he took my lamp and hid it. Then he shook my shoulder. "Are you asleep, young Ray?" I woke up with a jolt. I knew that, in wartime, it was a criminal offence to sleep underground.

"Oh, no, Mr. Knight. I was only resting my eyes".

146

"Were you, my boy? You must know where your oil lamp is, then. "

"Of course Mr. Knight" I said; and then I realized that it was nowhere to be seen.

Fred, my miner, came rushing back and tried to defend me, but it was no use. Mr. Knight said I would be reported to the police Pit Sergeant and taken to court. Unbeknownst to me, Mr. Knight had winked at Fred; and I was left to stew in my juice. I was too frightened to tell Dad.

Back at the coal face next morning, Mr. Knight , our colliery official and Fireman, took me to one side during one of his regular inspection rounds. He said, "Listen, young Ray. I don't want to report you for sleeping, and I don't think prison is suitable punishment for a lad of your age, so I tell you what I'll do; if you go to church every Sunday and join the choir, I won't report you for sleeping".

"But, Mr. Knight", I protested. "I already go to the Band of Hope in chapel once a week. Isn't that enough?"

"No, son, it's not. Band of Hope is fun: I'm talking about serious stuff."

I didn't say yes or no, so Mr. Knight continued on his rounds, and I resumed cutting and filling drams. I asked Fred what he thought . Being religious, he sided with Mr. Knight. "It's the lesser pain of the two, Ray. Try it for six months, and then you can stop." I went to see Fireman Knight at the end of the shift, and agreed to join the choir. So there I was, every Sunday, like a scruffy dirty angel, singing like a sparrow in my clean white surplice.

Leaving the church, there was always a gaggle of my mates making fun of me. I slowly came to the conclusion that it would have been better to have gone to prison, but I stuck it out – and I never fell asleep underground again.

The best political education anyone could get was when we stopped halfway from pit bottom to the coalface for a rest and a drink of water. There must be a better way forward than this rotten capitalist system we are under. High rates of child mortality- funeral after funeral passed through the village weekly. People died from TB, diphtheria, scarlet fever or chest infections. Hospital beds were in short supply, and 95% of people had no health cover, while the rich got the best care.

"We want socialism, and we want it now", was the call.

After my mam had died in childbirth, unable to get a hospital bed, this sounded like manna from heaven. Hope was in the air in 1945, with elections looming ever closer. That faint spark of hope was turning into a blazing beacon. We will nationalise our pits, we will work in safety. No more putting coal before pit props. Let's turn every capitalist monopoly into state owned enterprises for the benefit of all our people. I had a lot to say that night at the Young Communist League meeting. Dad never stopped nagging me about the YCL.

"Your brother George is not that stupid. Grandad and I helped form the Llanbradach Labour party branch. We will bring change with men like Bevan and Atlee. "

"But George did not look into our mam's eyes and see the pain, as she squeezed my hand. She didn't want to leave us", I said, the tears starting to flow. Dad turned away. He looked back.

"Your mam was beat, worn out. She would want you to look to the future, and not burden yourself with her death". I condescended to go out and deliver leaflets for the Labour

Party. The Communists, Trotskyists and our small band in the YCL worked together.

"Where are the Tories?" I asked dad one night.

"Oh don't you worry, son, they are only under cover. There are over 10,000 in our constituency."

"Not the miners!"

"No,", he said, "but backsliders, scabs, aspiring middle classes who think the working class does not have the intelligence to run the country. You can't see them, but they are there. They will always be there.

Back at the coal face, and the hard grinding toil, I was more than pulling my weight at cutting coal and filling drams. But my fellow boy miners and I could not wait for Saturdays. The bosses allowed us the concession to finish 1 ½ hours early, at 12:30, so we could go and watch Cardiff City play. To earn the early finish, we had to work twice as hard to fill our 4 or 5 drams. Fred Smith let me finish early for the matches on Saturday, even if we had only filled 2 drams, and, I always cut enough coal for the miner to fill it. The flip side of working Saturday mornings was that on Friday night, the miners let their hair down, and filled their bellies full of beer and cider.

It was impossible to have toilets underground, so when the call of nature came, you dropped your trousers where you worked and quickly covered it with a shovel of small coal.

The ventilating system meant that air came down one shaft, went through all the coal faces and back up shaft 2: so Saturday was particularly awful as the aroma of every miner's Friday night hung on the air. If I moaned about it, my miner would remind me that the miners' life was dangerous and hard. They deserved the chance to let off steam on a Friday night. "I know that", I said, "but it's the letting off steam on Saturday mornings that upsets my stomach".

Walking the two miles to pit bottom was always dangerous. There were no concessions made for safety. Dodging the journeys, the long line of coal trucks, was frightening. One young lad got jammed up against the side of the narrow tunnel. He lost an arm and never worked again. For a while we used to see him limping around Caerphilly town centre. After a while he left to work in a hotel in North Wales.

Sam Knight the Fireman stopped me at the coalface one day, and said, "I heard from your dad that you wanted a career."

"Oh, yes." I said.

"Well, your luck is in. The company is organising classes to train mining engineers. Can I put your name down?"

"Yes please", I said, thinking; what a great chance to get away from the daily grind and back to the once hated classroom. I waited patiently for two months. One pay day a letter came in my pay packet, telling me to report to the pit office at 6 the following Monday. I duly arrived at the office, armed with pen and paper, expecting a short induction course prior to starting training. Mr. Knight was there with another mining engineer. We sat down to a lecture on fire damp and the reasons for the horrific explosions at Senghenydd, which had killed 439 men and boys (including my relative) and Gresford. I was taking furious notes, but was baffled by the figures- fractions, trigonometry etc. "When do we start college, Mr. Knight?"

"College? College? There 's no college. You learn to be an engineer in your own time, not ours." That was the end of my aspirations to become a mining engineer. There were two reasons: my refusal to learn math's from my hated school teacher, who took great pleasure in caning and beating the living daylights out of me; and the fact that, by the end of my shift at the coal face, I was dead beat. I would be falling asleep – the math's and trigonometry which I didn't understand would have bored me to tears. It also would have meant missing out on my rugby, soccer and boxing training with the boys. Sam Knight had little time for me after that.

One day, as I was walking in with Fred and the other miners, a miner called Fred Wooton said, "You know, boys, we haven't had an accident for three weeks." Someone asked if he was keeping a log book of all accidents for the union lodge. "no" he said, " If I was, it would be filled 10 times over". I was speaking to the first aid man in the pub, and he told me how pleased the manager was because of the accident free weeks.

When we got to the face, we had to move two tons of rocks and other debris, the residue left from the shot firers' work on the previous shift. The day shift had to bore the hole for the shot firer. The shots man then expertly put just enough explosives to blow out a path of rock to allow the new lengths of dram rails needed for the drams to be pushed tight up to the coal face. It took us four hours to clear the debris , lay the rails and put a dram up to the coalface. The haulier who had brought the dram up with the horse had said to Fred, " If you can fill that one up quick, I will bring you another." Because we had already experienced a lean week of dram filing, our prospects of a decent wage were low.

"Come on, Ray", Fred said, "Let's fill this one quickly for the other dram".

"But Fred, I've already cut four pit props, and we should put them up especially after the shot fired on the previous shift".

"It won't take us twenty minutes, and then we'll both put the props in , fill the next dram and go home". We got stuck in, Fred on one side of the face, and me on the other, 15 yards apart. The dram was half full when there was an almighty crash. Dust flew everywhere. I pulled myself out of the rubble, bruised, and looked up the face, but I couldn't see six feet in front of me. I rushed towards where Fred had been working, and saw his legs twitching beneath a huge rock. I screamed at the top of my voice, and picked up the large stop wedge used to prevent a dram from running away. Using this and a sledge, I tried to prise the rock off Fred. By this time, the other miners had heard my shouts, and came rushing to help. We eventually pulled Fred out, but by that time he was dead. I lay down and cried like a baby. A miner put his arm around my shoulder and said, "Crying won't help, son, and your shoulder is bleeding quite badly." The word got around the whole pit, and everyone walked out.

When I reached the surface, I had to go straight to the first aid room. My arm and shoulder was bandaged, and I was taken by ambulance to Caerphilly Miners' Hospital.

"What, you again?" said the A & E doctor. "You've been crying boy - is it that painful?"

"Yes, it is", I said, "but that's not why I'm crying. I've not only just lost my miner, but my best friend. Tomorrow I have to face his wife and family, and tell them what happened. I'll have to tell them that if I had insisted on props before coal, Fred would still be here."

With that, the nurse bathed me, the doctor set my arm in plaster of Paris, and strapped my dislocated shoulder.

Eventually, I was back at the coal face. Nothing seemed the same without Fred Smith. I worked with a succession of miners for a few months. Then September came- hop picking time. Every year around this time, there was an exodus of miners from the coalface to Hereford. Not all the miners went, of course, because it was a punishable offence by law to absent yourself from the pit without a reasonable excuse, such as a doctor's note. It also meant taking children out of school, which again was against the law. Enough miners and their families went to create a drop in production.

Feeling quite down during that period, I and two other boy miners booked our places to pick hops in a farm just outside Ledbury, called Pool End. The appointed day of departure came; excited children in their Sunday best were sent to Llanbradach railway station to mind the piles of luggage. Most of the bedding, cups, plates etc were packed in large wooden tea crates, which when empty also served as a good hiding place for apples and pears stolen from the farmer. We brought back enough fruit to last our families until well after Christmas. The special train hired by the farmers (I think they used to deduct money from our hop picking earnings to pay for it) filled up quickly and went on its way to Herefordshire. A highlight of the train journey was going over the now demolished Crumlin viaduct. The train would slow down to five miles an hour, and there was a slight swaying as we went across. Girls looked down and screamed, and everybody cheered when we reached the other side in safety.

At Ledbury railway station, the farmers waited with large carts called gambos, on which they transported us all to the farmyard barns and cowsheds which would be home for the next fortnight. The women got stuck in scrubbing the cowsheds and barns, laying out the straw for bedding, using the tea chests for tables, and in no time the sheds were spick and span. Meanwhile, we boys and men gathered piles of wood for the communal fires on which all the cooking was done. Girls and boys slept in one large barn with a 12 foot high partition separating the sexes.

At night the girls would shout and invite us over:

"We....Want....To....Play!"

We answered,

"Be there in five minutes!" There were loud shrieks of laughter from the girls, but we boys were too frightened to climb the high barrier. We poached rabbits, and scrumped apples, pears, and plums from the farmer. Down on the hop fields, we ate rabbit stew with great hunks of bread.

Shouts of "Lardy cakes, lardy cakes! " brought us running with our pennies. I pledged true love for ever to Marlene Balinger. (I met her seven years later: she had two babies and had grown fat.)

The highlight of the month was the strike, demanding more money for picking a field of small hops. We all marched up from the fields singing Calon Lan and Cwm Rhondda. The gypsies, Marlene Ballinger and her gaggle looked on with amazement. The picket line formed outside the farm house. There were loud cheers from everyone when our delegation came out claiming victory: an extra 2d a bushel.

(50 years later, I visited the local pub in Ledbury with

Caerphilly Male voice Choir. Speaking to an old farmer, I bragged about our strike for more money. "We made you farmers pay." With a smile on his well lined face, he said,

'Oh, no, sir. We knew you would always have a strike during the month, and we deliberately left the smaller hops section until the last week, and kept the price of a bushel two pence below what we had agreed to pay. We appeared to give in to your demands and increase the amount per bushel by tuppence, and everybody was happy." I wondered whether our pit bosses did the same).

We came home from Hereford to face the music. One boy's parents were given a week in prison for allowing their child to miss a month's school; others were fined for being absent from the pit. We didn't care. The real profit for us was the healthy glow in the children's' cheeks and our suntanned faces, and our beautiful memories of singsongs in the Trumpet Inn, Pixley, and the friendships we made with the gypsies.

Back in work, the excitement was at fever pitch as the election was now just months away. Our Lodge reps were taking names for people to do political work in the Tory stronghold of Barry. I gave mine enthusiastically, and so once a week I was knocking doors. Most of the big houses gave us short shrift, but there was a good response from the Council estates.

The one ambition I had, after I was humiliated by the miners who refused to let me work with them, was to become the most sought after boy helper in the pit. My brother George had already achieved that status when he worked with Archie Isaacs from Bedwas, who was (wrongfully) called King of the Jews, and was well known for his betting on dogs. George was in his seventh heaven when he got his 5 shilling tip every payday.

Archie and his cross miner, Fred Wooton, had the top miners' job of driving the main heading in the Elliot district of the house coal pit. Fred had a boy miner working for him, so there was no opening for me. My chance came when his boy miner moved to another pit. I found out where Mr Wooton lived, and called around to see him. "Please, Mr. Wooton, can I be your boy miner?"

"There's not much of you, " he said, "and working with me is hard, very hard."

However, he did condescend to give me a trial run, and for the next month I worked my fingers to the bone. Fred seemed pleased with me, and so when my brother worked the main heading by day with Archie, I did the night shift with Fred, and vice versa. I had no trumps (tips) the first week, but the second week I earned 2 shillings, growing eventually to 6s, and took my place alongside my brother as the top boy miners in the pit.

At long last, the much talked about election took place. Fred Wooten and I were stuck into our work, cutting coal, filling 7 drams, putting up four huge timber posts on the heading, and putting up two gogs to mark a new stint (coalface) for another miner.

(Gogs are a series of short props criss-crossing one another, filled in with stone.)

We rushed to the pit bottom, where there was great excitement. Everyone was waiting for the last 20 drams of coal to go up the pit, which would release the cage for us to go up to the surface. "We are doing very well," said our mates who had arrived at the pit bottom before us, "We have taken Barry and 2 of the Cardiff seats". The next thing, a message came down from the 2 till 10 shift of miners.

"We have won the election by a landslide"! they shouted. There was a huge roar from the miners waiting to return to the surface. The hugging, the cheering and yes, the tears of joy seemed to go on forever.

"What are you crying for?" I asked Sam Norris.

"What the bloody hell do you think I'm crying for? We've won the right to build a future for our kids. Your mam died for the want of a hospital bed. Other mams coming from now on will get their beds. Our kids will get good schools and we will build the health service so long promised!"

When I got home, dad was up early from the night shift. He found it much easier than the day shift, with three of us working. After his night's hard graft at the coalface, he would get my brothers Leslie and William off to school, prepare dinner for the family, do the housework and shopping, and then grab 2 or 3 hours' sleep. How he managed it year after year, I'll never know. Dad told me in later years that he promised our mam on her deathbed that he would try and keep the family together. He tried hard to get my sister Joanie back from the a school for the deaf in England, and my sisters Vivian and Patricia from the Bridgend orphanage, but the authorities would not allow it. We were living in two rooms with my grandmother and cousin Iris. They told Dad that they would reconsider if he remarried, if there was a stepmother in the house. (One of the bonuses of having Dad working nights, and George working cross shifts, was that I could have the bath to myself.)

As I walked through the door , Dad was laughing, dancing like a mad jester. "We've won, We've won!" he shouted, "and we did it with our Labour party! We've won!"

"With a little help from the Young Communist league and the CP", I muttered.

"Yes," said dad, " but it was a Labour party manifesto, and we will change our lives for the better."

"Too late for mam", I said.

"Yes, but for millions of mams, for the sick and disabled, for peace and prosperity, a new dawn has broken".

I gave up the argument. I hugged my dad, something I had shrunk from in the past years. We laughed and cried, and I took the Labour party membership form from him, but never joined.

Underground, the bosses saw the writing on the wall and changed their attitude slightly. However, accidents still took place daily. Death was never far away, either in the pits or the community. My cousin Mary died at 16 years old, and another young cousin Eva died, aged just three. Dust was a big killer of the miners who had survived the death trap below ground. Most miners who gave their lives to King Coal died a horrible death, like my Dad, drowning in their own phlegm produced by lungs packed with fine coal dust. At last our big day came. The country's mines were coming under public control. We all moved up to the Lamp room. A ribbon was cut. Our Labour MP Ness Edwards and Harold Finch from the Lodge made emotional speeches. But the best of the day was from Dai Francis from the South Wales Miners' Union (Spanish Civil war veteran and father of Hywel Francis, who was elected MP for Aberavon). He said, "The fight for better pay and conditions must and will go on. The task is made much harder by the fact that the same bosses who have kicked us around over the years, who did their utmost to make capitalism work, have been given the job to nationalization work. On the apple trees are the fruits of freedom, of socialism, but it is only we, the workers, who can pick them." He was met with the loudest applause of the day. I thought my young hands were going to fall off with all the clapping, which I continued even after everyone else had stopped.

We went back to work at the coalface, cutting the coal, filling the 7 or 8 tubs, cutting props, laying dram rails, putting up flats. By now, George and I were earning top trumps (tips) from our miners for our unstinting work. We were both getting reasonable money, but I still feel, and always will, that boy miners were terribly exploited. At 17 ½ I was able to run the coalface on my own when my miner Fred Wooton took a shift off. I only needed 1 ½ drams to pay my wage, but I always filled four on my own. It was always profitable to employ a good boy miner. I had come a long way from the humiliation of being rejected by at least five miners on my first days underground at 14. I felt more than confident to run my own length of coalface;

the big problem for me was my accident rate.

Dad took me aside and said, "I think you should get out of the pit before you get killed". I was horrified. I protested that I was just ready to work my own coalface, and if I left the pit, I would be conscripted into the army. "Oh, no", said Dad. "You're undoubtedly unfit: bad eyes, bad chest, underweight. Go and see our doctor for an examination." At last I relented, and went to the doctor. He said there was no way I would be conscripted; I was definitely unfit. So I left Llanbradach Colliery to work in a local factory welding water tanks. I was so miserable: I missed the comradeship, the feeling of solidarity. Eventually I was called up for an army medical. At the end of an extensive examination, I asked the doctor if I was fit for army service. "Definitely not", he said. I went home and told Dad. I was just getting used to the factory work when my call up papers came through the door. "Report to Park Hall Camp, Oswestry, North Wales in five days."

I did my best to get back underground, but I ran out of time. Dad walked me up to Llanbradach railway station, gave me a hug, and said, "Sorry, son, I'm sure it's for the best."

During my two years fighting the Cold War, I was constantly in trouble for my leftwing socialist views. I was demobbed in 1950.

After two jobs working with Robert McAlpine and Staverton builders, I gave in to the pull of the mines, and got a job working in a drift mine just above Taffs Well. The work was still very hard, but we did have some mechanical aids. Coal still took priority, and after two accidents - one, where I narrowly escaped death when a buffer rope snapped, missing me by inches and killing my butty, I left and got another building job. I did a short spell at Nantgarw pit, but eventually got a good job in the steel industry. Two of my brothers, Leslie and William, were both invalided out of the pit. Billy had his leg amputated after being dragged out of a heavy fall of rocks. Leslie was trying to get to pit bottom when he was run over by a journey of coal drums. He tried to jump out of the journey's way, and his foot got caught in the rail points. George also left the pit through ill health.

There were many horrific explosions at Welsh pits, most notably the world's worst mining disaster at Senghenydd in 1913 where 440 lost their lives, at Gresford, and Nine Mile point. Accidents continued to happen. In Bedwas, as late as the 1950's, my second cousin had his ears burnt off, and his friend was killed at the scene of the explosion. My brief story mirrors many similar tales throughout the years; but out of the pain, suffering and death came giants of men, who broke the political mould. They, and our unions, eventually gave us that landslide victory in 1945 when we at last took control of our lives.

"All Out"

This video was found after almost thirty years in the house of one of our contributors, Dai (Ropey) Davies, he kindly lent us the only existing copy we know of. The discovery of this video led us to speak to Dr. Alex Clayton, head of film at Bristol University whose project it had been all those years ago. After converting it to DVD a copy was sent to him for the university's archives and he kindly gave us permission to use it. It will be shown at Big Pit as part of the 30 year commemoration.

There is a huge sense of solidarity about the whole film, everyone is making the best of what they have, below are some quotes from the video.

Christmas 1984 "It was a marvellous Christmas, she'll never beat us as a community, Maggie should come down and see for herself." A quote from one of the women from the Penrhiwceiber Womens Support Group.

"We know in South Wales that if we lose this fight it will be the end of our communities. We are fighting for our jobs and our boys coming behind us too. The spirit in Penrhiwceiber is like it was during the war. Our children will be able to look back on 1984 and say; 'Our parents fought for us,' with a sense of pride."

A Penrhiwceiber miner.

At one point in the film the women are remembering a march that they went on in Dover, they had support from the lesbians and gays and there was also a beautiful homemade red satin banner with the words, 'Black People support the Miners,' embroidered on. This support brought tears to the eyes of many of the women.

A lot of the film is dedicated to the giving out of food parcels, Christmas time they had extras such as mince pies, pickles, beetroot, corned beef and the lucky few also had a turkey. Many Christmas toys were donated for the children so that they didn't have to wake up with nothing on Christmas morning, which would have been terribly disappointing. In one scene they are reading out a letter from an old lady and her sister, it reads;

"We have great admiration for the stand that you are taking, for the NUM and the unions as a whole, best wishes and a happy Christmas to you all, we enclose a £10 donation and a £2 book of stamps;

From Mrs. Mable Hirst.

Many such letters were received along with donations and greeting cards. Dai (Ropey) Davies had this to say, "Lives lost in the mines run into hundreds, we've always had to fight. If a man died he'd be stretchered back to his house, whereas if a horse died there'd be a major enquiry. The women here have been outstanding, working and running the kitchens in an excellent manner. They have their own autonomy, without us interfering."

Throughout the film there are songs from The Mountain Ash RFC Choir, as well as children singing hymns during a church service.

Taken from the video 'All Out.'

The Role of the State

By the time the strike was over the miners had experienced at first hand the way in which the coercive power of the state can be, and is, used in defence of ruling class interests. The police, the judiciary, criminal courts and civil courts, even the D.H.S.S., were all used against the striking miners. No expense was spared: at a time when health, education and social services are being drastically cut some estimates of the cost of the miners' strike have been as high as £2,367 million. But as Nigel Lawson, the Chancellor of the Exchequer, explained to the House of Commons on 31st July 1984, it was a 'worthwhile investment' for the country – for the capitalist class that is.

That the coercive forces of the state should have been used against the striking miners, is not surprising. Governments – both Labour and Tory have used the police and even the army to break strikes many times before.

Reproduced with permission from The Socialist Party of Great Britain.
Extract taken from the pamphlet 'The Strike Weapon – Lessons of the Miners' Strike.'

Welfare Against the Workers

Of all the changes introduced by the 1980 Social Security Acts, Clause 6, which ordered a compulsory deduction to be made from the benefit payable to strikers' dependants, and which forbade the making of urgent needs payments to them and to single strikers, was the most pernicious and vindictive.

The government was elected, amongst other things, to restore a fairer bargaining balance between employers and trade unions. Clause 6 represents one of the steps taken to that end. Clause 6 was one of a number of preparations made by the Thatcher Government to defeat a long and protracted strike, and was shaped largely by what many Tories considered to be humiliations inflicted on the Heath Government by the miners' strikes of 1972 and 1974.

Frequently acknowledged as the vanguard of the organised working class, the miners were one of the groups identified by the right as potential opponents to their plans to transform British society. According to Alan Walters, Margaret Thatcher's chief economic advisor between 1979 and 1983, the Tory policy of dismantling the large nationalised industries was based on more than a belief in the virtue of so - called free market forces. It was also predicated on the belief that nationalised industries were a major stronghold of organised labour, and for that reason needed to be taken on. As Walters

173

put it, 'instead of commanding the nationalised industries, governments were largely commanded by them. The graffiti expressed it succinctly: **" Miners Rule OK?"**

Similarly, the final report of a Conservative Party policy group on the nationalised industries, leaked to *The Economist* in May 1978, revealed that 'the most likely battleground will be the coal industry' and added significantly: 'the greatest deterrent to any strike...would be to cut off the money supply to the strikers.' (Beynon,p.92/93)

These paragraphs are a part reproduction of the chapter 'Welfare Against the Workers' Jones C. and Novak T.

The following is a quote from Des who works at Big Pit:

"At last Maggie has joined the miners, now she's underground!"

PITS TO PARKS – A Poem by Julie Pritchard

I began to walk paths that miners walked to their place of work.
No pit head baths or men in camaraderie conversation, no
noise of their hobnailed boots marching in union to their daily
toil. I witness the sun shine away the dawn and listened to
nature in all its glory. A dawn chorus of coal tits, blackbirds,
wood peckers and the cry of the bird of prey. To moss lined
paths that were once tram lines, now idle railway sleepers that
have wild strawberries growing which are waiting to be picked.
Ogilvie Pit has gone, industry has turned to leisure. Tree lined
paths stare at the fluorescent flying cyclist whizzing past and to
walkers with no care. The earthy smell of the river Darran that
came from a stream far away, its brown back is snaking its way
to the river Rhymney. My footsteps mirroring my thoughts, as I
walk across to a wooded Valley to New Tredegar where Elliott's
Colliery once stood where the winding house still stands. The
entrance to the pit head is part of a cafe and an information
centre, a place to meet and eat. A far cry from the sixpence off
a miners pay that went towards the Miners Institute, where
books were read and a fountain of conversations were said, this

fed their thirst for knowledge for many were self taught. The Valley sides are a mass of purple from the heather to yellow gorse and blue black of the wimberries. The haunting sound, of the curlew, to tadpoles in ponds that fascinate the young, frighten others when they grow in to frogs. The air is cleaner now but let's not forget the miners who struggled to breathe with dignity, they had to leave this life before their time. The industrial remains recall the history of what was before, hidden for many years under the black coal mountains; the white swan of nature's beauty trying to lift its head, the aroma of the Buddleia shrub where butterflies flutter and caress this plant in thanks. Where miners once congregated there are benches to sit and reminisce. On I ramble to where three pits are now a country park, where a road goes over the top with a train station in the middle and a river runs through whirling, winding, colour gone from black to clear toffee brown. I have heard but not seen the otter, some say they are living along the green foliage banks, swimming by is the salmon and river trout. Standing in the river is the solitary, silent, serene figure of the fly fisher. Looking on is the stately heron waiting for its catch.

Blackberries, hazel nuts, sloes, a forager's paradise. No blackened figures of colliers going home after their hard shift at the face. Bargoed, Britannia and Pengam have long gone replaced by indigenous trees. To Penallta where the pit head baths has been replaced by a housing estate. A pit pony is engraved into the earth, paths that loop and link lead to circular walks. To a viewing platform to survey the present and past as you stand on soft coal grass. This journey brings me to south of the Sirhowy Valley a country park sits where nine mile point was, to Blackwood and the chartist bridge that spans in memory of the men who fought for the rights of the working man. To pits that were called Markham, Oakdale, Wyllie to Pochin colliery. To meadows where buzzing bees, rainbow of the wildflowers, to woods where the shy blue bell pokes its head out. I see a red kite floating on high, the ruddiness of its feathers adds colour to the bright blue sky. To a town that stands north of Sirhowy it was here in the beginning of the industrial revolution, with its earth filled with iron ore and coal. With its seventy two foot cast iron clock that stands passing time. The working class town called Tredegar.

Tranquil walks have replaced slag heaps, I look around me at the surrounding scenery that was once disguised as a spoil heap and sparse greenery covered in coal dust. Now it is an amazing sight where nature has reclaimed her own and has taken control and this brings peace to my soul.

Parc Cwm Darran on the site of the old Ogilvie Colliery which closed it's doors in 1975.

Bibliography

Beynon, Huw. Ed. *Digging Deeper: Issues in the Miners' Strike.* London: Verso, 1985.Print.

Beynon, Huw. "Engaging Labour: British Sociology 1945-2010," *Global Labour Journal: Vol. 2: Iss 1,* p. 5-26.

Griffiths, David. "Death of an Industry, Loss of Jobs and Communities in the South Wales Valleys." Aberdare College. 2010.

Jenkins. J.Geraint. *Getting Yesterday Right – Interpreting the Heritage of Wales.* Cardiff: University of Wales Press, 1992. Print.

"The Strike Weapon – Lessons of the Miners' Strike," *The Socialist Party of Great Britain.* 1985. Print.

Healy, Anthony. "Britain: The Ridley Report. How the Tories planned to take on the miners and the working class." 25th Feb. 2009.
<http://www.marxist.com/britain-ridley-report.htm>

Morris, Vicki. Aka Citizen Barnet. "The Tolpuddle Martyrs with the Miners." **<http://citizenbarnet.blogspot.co.uk/2010/07/honour-tolpuddle-fight-tories.html>**

Richards, Tim. "A Personal History of the Miners' Strike." *Planet, The Welsh Internationalist.* Winter 2010, Issue 197, p.30-35. Print.

Swain, Fay. Williams, Cory. Ed. *Penallta, A Brief History of Penallta, The last Colliery in the Rhymney Valley.* Researched and compiled by Lewis Girls' Comprehensive School. 1994. Print.

Striking Back, WCCPL & NUM (South Wales Area.) Welsh Campaign for Civil and Political Liberties and the NUM. 1985. Print.

Salt, Chris. Layzell, Jim. "Here We Go!, Women's memories of the 1984/85 Miners' Strike." Co-operative Retail Services Ltd. London. 1985. Print.

Printed in Great Britain
by Amazon